CROSS-COUNTRY SKIING

by

NED GILLETTE

with John Dostal

The Mountaineers
Seattle

THE MOUNTAINEERS: Organized 1906 ". . . to explore, study, preserve and enjoy the natural beauty of the Northwest."

Published by
The Mountaineers, 719 Pike Street, Seattle, Washington 98101

First printing October 1979, second printing December 1979, third printing January 1981, fourth printing October 1982

Published simultaneously in Canada by
Douglas & McIntyre Ltd., 1615 Venables Street,
Vancouver, British Columbia V5L 2H1

Published simultaneously in Great Britain by
Diadem Books Ltd.
85 Ballards Lane
London N3

Manufactured in the United States of America

Edited by Cynthia Mallory, designed by Marge Mueller

Cover photo: Author skiing below Mt. McKinley, Alaska. Photo by Galen Rowell

Library of Congress Cataloging in Publication Data

Gillette, Ned, 1945-
Cross-country skiing.

Includes index.
1. Cross-country skiing. I. Dostal, John, joint author
II. Title.
GV855.3.G54 1979 796.9'3 79-19415
ISBN 0-916890-88-0

Cross-country in the Northwest. (Van Brinkerhoff)

Contents

(Peter Miller)

INTRODUCTION

Other than an Olympic or World Championship event, the Holmenkollen in Oslo, Norway, is the most prestigious of ski games on the year's calendar. Fifty thousand spectators arrange themselves to shout frenzied encouragement along the 50 km cross-country race course. To win is to have reached the top of international racing; to participate was a realized dream for me on my first trip to Europe. At the sixth feeding station, manned by U.S. Team coach John Caldwell, the track was downhill just enough to keep me gliding. Skiing through a corridor of vocal Norwegians who surely discerned that my inexperienced body was beginning to burn out, I eagerly took the cup of energy-laden liquid from John's extended hand. With a sweeping motion worthy of a champion beer chugger, I reared back, the better to throw the drink directly down. Too far! One ski was launched into the air, sweeping above my head as I, like a drunk slowly crumbling, landed neatly on my rear in front of my first international audience.

This memory kept recurring as I considered adding my own book on cross-country to those already on the shelves. Why another one? It seems to me that other books assume you'll take the nourishment they offer in one neat gulp. My experience teaching, racing, and expeditioning suggests that it often goes over the shoulder or down the chest, or that occasionally, like me, the skier is airborne in the process. I've yet to find a book fully realizing that, as my colleague John Dostal says, "When you take technique off the page and onto the snow, it can be a pretty messy process." Along with descriptions and demonstrations of competent skiing, you'll find in the pages that follow as much on what can go wrong and what to do about it as what is right, and some exercises and suggestions on how to get a feel for the maneuvers — in short, not just ideal execution but what you'll really need to know to be comfortable on your skis and clever on the trail.

The Trapp Family Lodge in Stowe, Vermont, was the first major cross-country ski center in the United States.

Today it is one of the premier centers in the world (though, contrary to popular belief, we do not accompany our lessons with tunes from "The Sound of Music"). The Trapp ski school is unique because it employs people who lead their lives on the premise of serious enjoyment, especially of skiing, where each has established an area of expertise. In drawing from this deep well of experience, as well as from previous teaching at ski schools in Colorado and California, I've been able to write about skiing from a practical point of view, to help you cope with learning technique, weather, terrain, and snow conditions, and to understand proper equipment and clothing and the mysteries of waxing.

Since over the years we've been able to anticipate people's problems and develop useful solutions, I've included many anecdotes from the hundreds of lessons taught at Trapp's. I hope there is something in this book for all levels and interests of skiers, whether you're a racer, a tourer, or a mountaineer.

Perhaps a word to explain John Dostal's contribution to this book is in order. It is simply this: the final revision of the manuscript was as much John's as mine. What began as a critical reading of an emerging text turned into happy collaboration. Toward the end of this business of writing,

Not bad technique for six-year-old Sam Von Trapp. (Ned Gillette)

Cross-country is more than skiing on the flat. (Ned Gillette)

not only did I need an editor of John's caliber to cut through the morass of words and overlapping ideas in which an author can easily get bogged down, I also needed someone to look at the sport through a different set of eyes to guarantee accuracy and clarity. John supplied this different window, as well as contributing a good deal of original material both technical and anecdotal. After a winter spending "days off" ensconced in my writing grotto when I not surprisingly would have preferred to be out *doing* the skiing, it was a joy to sit with John and laugh our way through a springtime month of final rewriting. This book would not be the same without his contribution.

Photographs tell the story as much as, often more than, words. Here I turned to one of the best ski photographers working: Peter Miller provided nearly all the sequence photos and is directly responsible for the pictures clearly describing what is being explained in the text.

The two truly unsung heroes of the book are Allan Bard and Audun Endestad. Allan is a mountaineer and Audun is a racer, but both have a marvelous ability to describe the hows and whys of skiing maneuvers and equipment in the most understandable phraseology I've yet heard — they are experts in that most difficult of arts: communication. I spent many hours of discussion with them, and the fruits are boldly incorporated in the following pages. Stacy Studebaker helped with the chapter on teaching kids. Finally, Mountaineer Books Director John Pollock and editors and designers Rebecca Earnest, Donna DeShazo, Cynthia Mallory, and Marge Mueller — their great contributions all too easily overlooked — were indispensable for advice and revision.

My thanks to Wayne Merry, Jack Miller, and Beverly Johnson for pointing my restless energy toward the mountains and to Doug Wiens for continuing it; to Don Henderson, Bill Clough, Al Merrill, John Caldwell, and Marty Hall for guiding me through the years of racing; to Johannes von Trapp for the confidence to run a ski school in a uniquely creative way; to Mike Brady and Galen Rowell for the encouragement to go ahead and write; and to my parents for starting me on skiing at the age of three and keeping the faith that their son would eventually find a way to combine life's work and play.

Skis can take you to such wilderness as Don Sheldon Amphitheater, near Moose's Tooth in Alaska. (Ned Gillette)

1
SKIING TODAY

Skiing evolved from the necessity of traveling in winter. Nordic or cross-country skiing began in the rolling terrain of the Scandinavian countries primarily to get from one village or hunting cabin to another. The lightness of the equipment and the graceful speed of movement it allowed came from the need to pass over the countryside as quickly as possible. Alpine or downhill skiing developed in the Alps, to enable people to negotiate the steep mountainous

Cross-country outside your back door. (Peter Miller)

slopes of central Europe. Its equipment evolved in quite a different direction, sacrificing lightness and free movement on the flats for maximum control in downhill descents.

Nordic and Alpine skiing, long considered by many to be totally separate, are now drawing closer as Nordic skiers develop new techniques and expertise to handle difficult downhills on their cross-country skis, revive old turns like the telemark to compensate for loose-heeled bindings, and design metal-edged skis and heavier boots for increased control on the downhill slopes. Some Alpine skiers are freeing themselves from lift-served skiing and moving toward cross-country through ski mountaineering and Alpine touring. Ski ascents of untouched peaks followed by runs through slopes of seemingly endless virgin powder are filling them with delight as they rediscover the joys of the wilderness.

As Nordic and Alpine increasingly overlap in both technique and philosophy, it is becoming apparent that what separates them is primarily a difference in the equipment used. The common ground shared by the two styles of skiing is that they both supply challenging exercise to a nation becoming more aware of physical fitness and offer access to the secrets of a world locked under winter's wraps.

Skiing is skiing, and to judge Alpine against Nordic is unnecessary. Many of us thoroughly enjoy both styles of skiing, combining the skills, merely choosing the proper equipment for the terrain to be encountered on different treks. I have chosen to describe no Alpine and little ski mountaineering equipment in this book, but all of the techniques described in the chapter on skiing downhill are as applicable to Alpine skiing as to cross-country, as are the observations on how to learn a new activity, how to cope with terrain, weather, and snow, how to approach racing mentally, and how to survive if forced to spend a night out in the winter.

The growth of ski touring centers in North America is exciting because it presents an opportunity for ordinary humans not living near the prepared tracks of a college or high school ski team to feel the exhilaration of faster track skiing. As the expansion of citizens' ski racing follows the

In the big mountains on cross-country skis. (Galen Rowell)

jogging craze, those who never before considered themselves athletes are looking at new horizons as they line up for the starting gun. And this social aspect of cross-country in no way inhibits those who wish to venture off on their own as solitary travelers drifting through the silence of winter, or the ski mountaineer challenging the unforgiving crags.

The Nordic expertise which was brought across the Atlantic from Europe has taken years to disperse throughout North America. In the early days skiing was almost totally dictated by terrain — Scandinavian in the rolling hills of the East and Midwest, and Alpine in the big mountains of the West. But East and West have met, and each has helped the other in a broad growth of the sport. Due to Western influence, ski mountaineering is gathering converts in the racing and track-oriented East, while racing, track skiing, and the use of light equipment is gaining a strong foothold in the West alongside mountaineering.

Today cross-country skiing is a blend of jogging, pure track speed, Alpine skiing, and backpacking, giving us four sports in one. The beauty of cross-country is that there is something in it for everyone. You can do it fast or slow, over long or short distances, through easy or difficult terrain, socially or alone, in groomed tracks or bushwhacking. Cross-country skiing is a multifaceted adventure. Tourers can go a flat, slow kilometer and reap the same sense of satisfaction as the daredevils flying down a tree-speckled, powder-laden slope. The racer-scientist can wax skis to perfection while the casual skier can hitch on a pair of waxless no-hassle boards.

Make of it what you wish, and enjoy it for what it is for you. No matter how fast, how far, or how hard you ski, relaxed yet focused skiing is what you're after. In a world that speeds on at an ever-accelerating rate, we all need the relaxation of the woods and meadows; of adventurous expeditions; of low-key competition; of the freedom of skiing across the countryside.

2

GETTING STARTED

The cold wind that occasionally blows across the meadow in front of the Trapp Family Touring Center surprisingly seems to blow away students' anxieties about being on skis for the first time. Both instructors and students are united in their desire to get into the sheltering woods 200 yards away. With no formal instruction, only frosty imitation, students produce a fast shuffle before they have a chance to worry about which hand moves with which foot.

Once you have overcome the first barrier and gotten onto your skis, however, learning basic technique will dramatically increase your enjoyment of skiing. Cross-country has always been promoted in North America with the promise, "If you can walk, you can ski." But the skier kicking and gliding past you will surely suggest something more than walking. And it is pretty unusual to ski on terrain that doesn't have uphills, downhills, and corners, each of which calls for a different kind of skiing. A vast majority of the skiers I see at touring centers would enjoy skiing infinitely more if they worked with a good instructor for an hour or two. That's all it would take. I still need coaching, why not you? Asked if he still got technical coaching, U.S. Ski Team member Stan Dunklee said, "Not so much anymore, but I'll still consider carefully anything anyone has to say about my technique."

To me, learning how to enjoy skiing and get over the snow is much more important than the equipment you use or the wax you apply. Therefore, you'll find this technical information at the end of the book. I'd suggest renting skis, boots, and poles while you are learning, and investing in your own equipment later.

If you are of sound mind and body, you should expect to get around fairly proficiently after a lesson or two. But how many more after that? There's no firm answer to this

Untracked snow is a real joy. (Michael Brady)

question. Some skiers thrive on a week's worth of daily lessons while others need time to find out on their own how their skis work. One young man turned up repeatedly for lessons to help him get into citizens' racing. It was finally suggested that a 25th lesson (honestly!) would be a lot less helpful than jumping into his first race. Instruction can enhance your experience but should not isolate you from it.

What are the basics that you need to know? Eventually you need to know all the maneuvers possible to negotiate all types of terrain and snow. You may not be interested in becoming a racer or a ski mountaineer, but you do need the fundamentals which allow you to be efficient and not waste energy, to handle terrain effectively, and to survive in practical situations you'll meet out on the trail every day of your skiing life.

To get the most out of your lessons, choose a learning environment that is nonstressful. Ski with an instructor you like and respect, and take a private lesson if that makes you more comfortable than learning in a group. Make sure the snow and weather conditions are good (ice and deep snow are difficult). Machine-groomed slopes and tracks really speed learning; that's why all the following demonstration photographs are of track skiing — it is easier for you to see clearly what's happening, although the maneuvers are applicable to off-track skiing as well. In this controlled environment you easily experience the feeling of increasingly better strides and turns. The more you practice, the more likely you will instinctively ski well when the going gets tough out on the trail.

Since all of us can absorb only so much new information before we are saturated, it's best at the beginning to keep things simple. For instance, all you really have to do to ski correctly on the flat is to be in a good stance, develop a good rhythm, angle your poles back for push, and have your weight on your forward ski as you stride. This will get you skiing 80 percent correctly, and the other 20 percent of perfection can come with practice.

There is no established way of teaching which will ensure a smooth stride or a perfect downhill turn for everyone. Different people respond to different exercises and different ways of explaining things, and what makes sense to you may not to the next person. A good instructor is

Gaining some speed makes cross-country skiing a totally different sport – and adds excitement. (Peter Miller)

familiar enough with skiing to present the same point or maneuver in several different ways in order to get you to understand and feel what is going on under your skis and to relate skiing to your experience.

There are certain activities with which most North Americans are familiar, like jogging, riding bicycles, playing tennis, catching a football, skateboarding. I like to teach skiing by drawing analogies to these easily understood activities. For example, ski on the flat in the body position you would take to receive a tennis serve. In learning, a mental picture is truly worth a thousand words of explanation.

An instructor may at times make a point via a "negative" approach so we can feel for ourselves how difficult we make some activities. To correct an error, it helps to exaggerate it to the extreme, to ski really wrong. For example, if your knees are not flexed enough, try skiing with absolutely stiff and straight knees to see how awkward it is. Now flex them more to feel the forward release of productive energy. We often do not know what is right unless we can feel what is wrong. A good instructor will serve as a mirror in which to see yourself objectively, able to mimic your every skiing movement precisely, especially your errors. Compare this with a demonstration of correct technique and the difference will be obvious. It's the next best thing to using a video camera.

Don't be a passive sponge when learning. If you don't feel comfortable skiing down a hill, say so. The instructor is there for you, not the other way around, and it's his or her job to be aware and creative in teaching you.*

The very best teacher is imitation. Jump into the track directly behind your instructor (who will be skiing at an easy pace) and match him stride for stride. Absorb his rhythm. Notice the subtle motions he uses to cruise comfortably over the snow. Be like a five-year-old when you learn to ski — open and absorbent. "No lesson!" trumpets young Sam von Trapp, who skis regularly with Trapp instructors. If he wants to go up a hill, he won't ask for a detailed explanation but will watch closely as you do it. He is a wonderfully sly learner.

Occasionally students have introduced themselves to their instructors by announcing, "I want you to know that you're dealing with a klutz." For these people and for the instructor there is heavy psychological weather ahead. It is not very helpful at the beginning of a lesson to get down on yourself. This will only short-circuit your progress. So will competing with the other students or your instructor, assuming that you can learn all of cross-country skiing in a day, or concentrating on your failures and forgetting your successes.

A successful businessman from New York came to the Trapp Family ski school outfitted with the latest racing gear and expecting to become an expert skier in a week of intensive instruction. His expectations so greatly exceeded what was possible in the time he had given himself that he

*Skiers and instructors alike come in both the male and the female mode. I've tried to make the language reflect this as much as possible; sometimes I've failed.

For better skiing, match your instructor stride-for-stride. (Michael Brady)

became unwittingly unreceptive to learning and made little progress — leading to an acute case of frustration. His problem was compounded by a sense of being always on display. When we were out skiing together, as soon as another Trapp instructor approached he promptly fell off his skis, probably thinking, "There's another one who is going to see how poorly I ski!" The second instructor had no idea that he had been called for jury duty. To help our student understand the bind he had put himself in, we asked if he could make us shrewd and successful investment bankers in the same time period.

For many skiers the words "falling" and "failing" not only sound alike but equal each other. As soon as backside touches snow, the self-indictment begins. Much better to remember that snow is nontoxic, and try to focus on *why* you fell: look at the track your ski made, remember where you were looking or where your hands were. Students who have fallen on downhills will often be asked by an instructor, "Where were your hands?" Often a quick, protective, "In the wrong place," is the response. But what the instructor is after is physical focusing, not psychological judgment. The skier who is relaxed enough to say, "It felt as if they got behind me," is making an important discovery about skiing. If good skiers were to get down on themselves every time they took a wind-milling half-gainer at high speeds, they'd be too depressed to wax their skis for another day's run!

Another day's run (call it insightful repetition) is just what is needed. You don't have to be in a class to tune up your own skiing but just have to have a willingness to go back over a section of a trail that may have thrown you, practicing and changing your approach until you have mastered it. "You make it look so easy. I feel sort of unbalanced being on one ski at a time," says the despairing student to the instructor, who may ski daily and takes an off-season vacation on skis. "And why not?" replies the instructor. "You've been on skis for all of ten minutes." Remember the first time you drove an automobile? Was your timing a bit shaky in traffic? So too in learning to ski: there is simply no substitute for getting kilometers under your skis. And you have to prevent your expectations from boiling over while you're accumulating the distance, perfecting your technique so you feel comfortable on your boards in all trail conditions and instinctively do things right. How do you eat an elephant? One bite at a time.

A less experienced instructor once said to me, in difficult 32°F./0°C. snow when the ski trails were rutted and apt to throw one off balance: "Ned, how can you ski so easily in this chop? How do you know when to shift techniques and speeds?" My response was not that I was a better athlete but that I'd probably skied 10,000 more kilometers than he had, producing instinctive reactions to the situation at hand.

Progress is relative for all of us. Getting a little jogging action on the flats may provide the beginner or casual skier with all the speed desired, while the marathon foot runner aspiring to equal past road-running times will be striving for much more, as will the ex-Alpine racer who tries to carve high speed turns on skinny skis, or the hard-core backpacker who wants to trek through the wilderness in winter. Levels of expertise must be measured by your own standards. What is possible for one skier may not be for another, and expectations that are presently beyond reach only lead to frustration. Not being able to do a parallel turn doesn't mean you cannot have fun on cross-country skis. Also, it's remarkable how agile and coordinated everyone is in some aspect of skiing. One woman was distressed that she couldn't learn to snowplow as fast as others in her class. She had to be reminded that, if she wanted to keep score, she was at the head of the class in skiing uphill and the only one that coordinated the difficult kick double-pole.

It is useful occasionally to take things apart and monitor your skills as you ski. Think of it as a checklist or tune-up. Take things one at a time, focusing on hands, body position, leg movement, and so forth.

Over-analysis, however, can be as much of a problem as careless skiing. Instructors will often pull up alongside a student grimly immersed in the solemn process of learning, lean over, and brightly suggest, "Smile." You are having fun! Don't keep pulling up the turnips to see how they're growing! Avoiding excessive analysis is especially important on downhill, and you may want to try relaxing by using tricks like wiggling your toes in your boots or holding your poles really lightly in your hands. Facial relaxation — relaxing your tongue and lower jaw — may allow natural body movement to occur. Look around. Was that a gorgeous birch tree you just passed? Sing your favorite song as you ski. Singing sets a cadence and quiets the mind. Try waltzing down the trail to "Around the World in Eighty Days"!

None of these tricks is really propelling you down the trail, but they do take your mind off trying to analyze and overthink every motion. The result is that your body can perform as it is capable. When I'm skiing really well, I'm sensing my overall motion forward, not any of the individual ingredients which make up that motion. So instead of trying desperately hard to ski well, much of the time we should just let ourselves go and ski. J.C. Killy explains it: "What has happened is that the excitement or challenge of

Remember to relax – smiling helps! (Ned Gillette)

the moment has captured your attention, freeing your mind from conscious thought of the complexity of the task you are performing."

A couple of years ago I had several good race results over competitors who were younger and better trained than I. Why? I hadn't raced much for ten years, and I was in only moderate shape. Yes, I did have years of experience to draw upon, but the main reason for success was that I was loose and at ease, skiing with relaxed concentration to utilize all my available energy. Because I was racing for the fun of it with no great expectations, I could fully enjoy my successes and my mistakes out on the race course. I was skiing my own race, skiing only for myself. (This didn't prevent me from talking to other competitors as we sped through the race. I encourage those I pass, and especially those who pass me.)

I've heard many observers of cross-country (particularly of an Alpine persuasion) say that it is a monotonous, dull, plodding sport. If you do ski walking only, it may be. But once you get the feeling of momentum carrying you down the trail, of being up and over your skis, of gentle and secure forward speed, it is a totally new sport with a subtle, gravity-defying fluidity: the more speed, the greater sense of release — even true on uphills where, with a little extra effort, you can scamper up lightly. The Alpine skier, accustomed to cruising at 20 mph, will be in for a pulse-quickening surprise at the same speed on skinny skis.

Speed becomes less scary as you become more experienced. Everything seems to slow down. You seem to have more time to make turns. Instead of merely hanging on, hoping to get through a difficult section without crashing, you are looking ahead and anticipating how you can at least maintain and possibly increase your speed. You begin to feel more powerful, more in control, and as if you are skiing the trail rather than the trail skiing you.

I'll be learning to ski for the next 35 years, just as I have for the past 35. There is always something to discover or perfect. I find new challenges and more enjoyment in the sport with each passing year. Fortunately we're all students, regardless of proficiency. One of my friends says racing keeps him honest and is good for his teaching since it puts him in the position of a student: everything must be executed well at higher speeds and a higher pulse rate when there may be confusion and frustration to deal with. In the same way, skiing Alpine-area trails on light cross-country equipment is a real tonic to sharpen interest for skiers whose local touring trails are getting too familiar. For me, ski mountaineering expeditions provide the challenge to infuse new spirit into my skiing — no trip is like any other, each requiring innovative research and planning, specialized equipment, new skiing and climbing talents, and in-the-field resourcefulness to assure success. Learning is an on-going process for everyone.

3

CROSS-COUNTRY FOR KIDS

Cross-country is a great family sport — available, affordable, and full of shared experiences and challenges like making it to the top of the ridge for a picnic and the annual family snowball fight, followed by the cannon ball derby on the descent. But how do you get kids started so you can all really ski together?

Some parents who deliver their kids to the Trapp ski school may assume that they have secured an hour of formal instruction for the child. But the shared grins of child and instructor should torpedo this belief: they're going off to play in the snow. There'll be plenty of learning to be sure, but it won't be forced. These are some ways we go about it. Try them for yourself if you're a competent

Getting acquainted. (Peter Miller)

Games help keep it fun. (Doug Wiens)

skier and have fun with kids. If you're a beginning skier yourself and want everyone in the family to have a lesson, let the kids ski in a group with others of the same age.

Start kids out on easy terrain with flats, bumps, little hills, and tracks for easy sliding and striding. Above all don't teach too much; let them discover skiing for themselves, using their considerable abilities as imitators. Use plenty of games — almost anything that works on grass will work on snow: red light-green light, tag, soccer, hockey, foxes and hares, relay races, follow the leader. Not only do children have a short attention span, but they'll get tired as well. So give them a break and have some fun yourself by giving them a ride, towing your little ones uphill or along the trail by having them hold onto your extended ski pole. They'll quickly get a sense of riding a gliding ski, of what happens when they lean forward or back. Older children can make a chain of ski poles, looping straps around baskets. Space them out so they won't ski

Top to bottom: Simon says, "Bob up and down." Sneaking along. Lending a hand with the pole pull. (Peter Miller)

over each other, and tow the whole bunch. Or put a child between your legs, holding onto your knees, with the little skis in the track and the big ones outside as you double-pole. Many kids like a good push at the end so they can do some free sliding.

Don't get technical. Skiing is a natural activity for children, and it's pretty likely that they aren't concerned with a lot of the hangups that adults are, like falling over, or the proper rhythm for making turns downhill (chances are it's more thrilling to bomb the slope straight, anyway). The two skiers in the middle photograph are skiing well for five-year-olds — or any age, for that matter. They haven't been told to get their weight out onto the forward ski but instead are doing some sneaking, creeping up on a larger skier. Don't worry if your kids end up doing something besides what you had intended. As long as they're out in the snow, they're learning and discovering things for themselves. Be available to lend encouragement, but don't hover about in a heavy-handed way.

Children will discover downhills on their own and will relish falling a good deal more than you do. All you may need to do is help extract one of them from a snowbank and provide an occasional lift back up the hill, but a bit of instruction on how to get up after a fall will produce real confidence to try new things. Squatting on their skis as they move downhill will keep kids close to the snow and secure. They can push off and do some paddling with their hands, and then, in a "Simon says" fashion, bob up and down until they're finally comfortable on their skis.

With very small people or ones that are not having much fun on downhills, you might try holding the child in front of you, his skis running straight as yours snowplow in a wide wedge. This way the child will glide securely and you can keep him in balance, letting go for longer periods as confidence builds. Kids won't respond very well to a lecture on how to turn, but set up a slalom course with ski poles if slalom poles aren't handy, start to snake down yourself, and watch them turn as they begin to follow you. Limbo events and a natural or constructed jump are real attractions for the close-to-the-snow crowd.

Many of the children in the accompanying photographs are learning to ski in a school program begun by interested

"Armpit aid" turns initial security into self-sufficiency. (Peter Miller)

Slalom courses teach coordination. (Peter Miller)

parents. With a little professional help in the beginning from instructor Stacy Studebaker, the program was self-sufficient in the second year. If your child is a preschooler, he or she still may be ready for skiing — three years old may not be too early for sliding and tumbling. If it seems to be, how about a trip on a ski-pulled sled?

You don't need much of an outlay in either clothes or equipment to get them started. According to the Hamilton sisters (ages six and nine) of Moscow, Vermont, "Beginners should wear proper clothes like snowpants and sweaters and a jacket or vest to go skiing." You don't need to bundle them up until movement is nearly impossible, but you should dress them with anticipation of plenty of time rolling in the deep stuff whether in cold Vermont or soggy Oregon. Waxless skis are great for kids, or, if you use waxable skis, make sure they are well waxed to ensure enjoyment. Shorter rather than longer skis make playing and maneuvering second nature. For really little ones a simple leather strap binding that can be worn with their own winter boots is all you need. For these younger, shorter skiers, poles will only be an encumbrance. Don't worry about older kids outgrowing skis, boots, and poles — there always seems to be a market for second-hand equipment, and many communities have a ski swap in the fall.

As kids get a bit older, encourage them to enter a few races. Not only can this be fun if approached in the right way, but a bit of competitive peer pressure will often supply the interest and challenge necessary for kids to want to stay with this outdoor sport.

Low-key racing for the fun of it. (Ned Gillette)

Skiing Ellesmere Island. (Allan Bard)

4

FREE AND EASY ON THE FLAT

The diagonal stride is really cross-country skiing's emblem: a skier stretched out on the flat, gliding in easy defiance of gravity. But learning it (or teaching it) isn't always that easy. Either you are told again, "If you can walk you can ski," which is reassuring but often produces no more than a ponderous shuffle, or you can furrow your brow over the kinesthetic diagrams in the latest coaches' manual. But fortunately there's a middle way: simply start by jogging on your skis.

If you're a newcomer to the sport, you'll probably start out shuffling, standing straight up and down like a stick figure and hesitantly advancing one ski and foot forward. After the tippy novelty has worn off, try leaning forward a little bit as if leaning into a strong wind. Notice how much

At first, get a feel for short jogging strides and leaning forward on your skis. (Peter Miller)

more your skis glide and how much less work you're doing. If you start out with your body slumped over a bit, as if you are about to receive a tennis serve or catch a football in your stomach, you will remain comfortably forward and in good balance on your skis. For proof positive, return to the stick-figure style, which will already feel a bit ungainly. Continue to lean forward, but put the same sort of spring into it that you put into jogging. As John Dostal observes, it's more like springing across a stream than simply putting a tentative foot out as you step off a curb. You're committing your whole body to the forward effort, and what you land on is not the jogger's asphalt road but a platform sliding on the snow.

We've left you balancing on one foot gliding along. How do you obtain a grip in this slippery stuff to continue jogging? A rubber sole is secure on asphalt in the summer, but what about these skis?

Listen to a seven-year-old friend of mine explaining things to an obvious first timer: "See, all you have to do is put a little pressure on your skis as you go forward." Here in one short sentence of simplicity and sophistication is the essence of diagonal striding. I considered resigning in the face of such brilliance!

This pressure is what is usually called kick. When your weight is on the forward, gliding ski, press (kick) down on it so it will grip the snow, providing a platform from which to "launch" yourself onto the other ski that is coming forward — a skier's form of jogging. Many beginners think that what makes you move forward is only a "scootering" or pushing back with one ski, but you need to press down for grip first. Think of how you would jog on a slippery, snow-covered road, pressing down when your weight is directly over your forward or kicking foot for maximum traction.

Now try to put it all together, jogging with a steady rhythm. Avoid any distinct hesitation at the end of each stride. You don't "freeze" at the end of each stride as you run down the street, do you? A good way to feel this rhythm is to follow a good skier who is skiing slowly, matching strides. Or try jogging up a moderate hill as if you didn't have skis on. This will speed up your rhythm to a point where you can't think every segment of your stride through to complicated disaster and will give you more security if you're worried about catapulting over the tips of your skis. I've found this "speed-up" exercise to be a sure cure for many cross-country errors and prescribe it repeatedly for students of all abilities.

No-Pole Work

To improve rhythm and balance, try skiing without poles, letting your hands pull you out over your skis and down the track. You'll have one less piece of equipment to

Learn the rhythm of cross-country without poles. (Peter Miller)

With practice, you'll be able to lengthen your stride and increase your speed. (Peter Miller)

think about. Allow your arms to swing back and forth comfortably to set your tempo, keeping your hands relatively low in front. If you can see them up in front of your face, they're too high and will throw you back off your forward ski instead of pulling you onto it.

Although you see experienced skiers swooping down the track with long strides, at first stick to a short jogging stride which will make steady rhythm easier to maintain. Long strides will lead to bad habits in the beginning, the most prominent of which is setting your weight too far back so that your hips are behind rather than over your front foot and ski. After all, you don't jog with a 10-foot stride, do you? Many beginners notice the tail of an experienced skier's rear ski lifting high off the snow, and try to copy it. This is simply the follow-through from leaning forward over a kick which is powerful, just as you'd follow through in a sweeping arc after hitting a tennis ball. In time this longer stride and leg follow-through will develop naturally.

Don't kid yourself, it is undeniably hard to stand on a narrow ski as it scoots down the track; but it will quickly

become easier with practice and if you ski in machine-made tracks at a touring center.

Weight

As you ski you will discover that the secret in cross-country is feeling where your weight is on your skis for different types of terrain. Weight too far off the center of your skis will slow you, tire you, or cause you to fall. Weight that is not over your feet will cause you to slip on the uphills, set you back awkwardly on the flats, prevent turning on the downhills, throw you out of each corner, and make each bump or dip in the trail a major obstacle. Cross-country becomes easy only if you are right on your skis.

Weight shift game: Instructor Gene Drake teaches via a series of clever games. Here's the one he likes best for quickly giving you a feeling of momentarily maintaining balance on one ski with control (which is the foundation for competent skiing and necessary for diagonal striding,

The ability to balance on one ski is essential. (Peter Miller)

switching from one track to another, stepping around trees, and so forth).

Find a long, straight section of trail with just enough pitch to let gravity provide some forward momentum. While gliding in the tracks, lift one ski slightly off the snow. Put it down and lift the other ski. Continue to alternate skis and try to increase the time spent easily on one ski.

Skating on skis: One of the best ways I know to feel a definite weight shift from one ski to the other is to skate on skis. Here you'll be forced to throw your weight from ski to ski as you push off like a speed skater. This will already be familiar to Alpine skiers, who will find it easier on X-C equipment.

Select a flat or ever-so-slight downhill packed area. Start by striding forward in your ordinary diagonal stride. Once you are moving, let your ski tips splay out in a "V." Edge your skis to the inside (that is, roll your ankles to put your weight on the inside edges) and push off one, then the other, with a constant rhythm. Give yourself an additional double-pole push with each stride.

Skating gives you a feel for rhythm and weight shift. (Peter Miller)

Bend knees to shift weight: Not only is it noisy slapping the track as your back ski comes forward, but it is unnecessarily brutal on you and on your ski. It is caused by having your weight too far back. Since some skiers feel insecure balancing on one ski, they shift their weight too early onto the ski coming forward. This error is prevalent with those who have learned to ski while carrying heavy backpacks, where they need their weight equally on both skis for stability.

Many track skiers, even those with years of experience, diagonal-stride with blocked or stiff hips, caused by straight or stiff knees. The term "blocked" means the hips don't come forward with the gliding or forward ski, or back with the kicking leg. The result is reduced extension in the stride, little power in the kick, little uphill grip, little momentum, and only slight weight shift onto the gliding ski.

Weight shift is accomplished by loosening your hips. To loosen hips and stretch out your stride, simply bend your knees or lower your stance a little as if you were receiving a tennis serve.

To prove to yourself how stiff knees block your entire

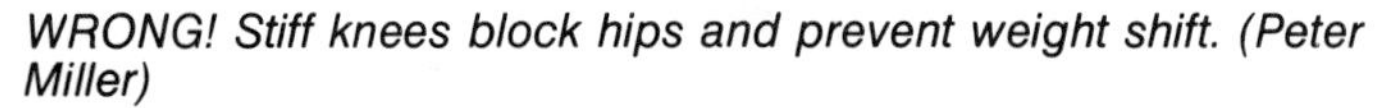

WRONG! Stiff knees block hips and prevent weight shift. (Peter Miller)

technique, simply try to ski with locked knees and feel what it does to your movements.

If you're still having problems loosening up your hips, think of "poling through your hip" with each stride. As your arm pushes back, your hip comes forward.

Another way to get the feeling of weight shift is by jogging up a gradual hill with skis. Here decreased speed and increased tempo will allow you to bounce more completely onto the forward ski.

If you are slipping more than others when you ski and not getting your skis to grip the snow, it can be for one of several reasons:

1. Wrong or insufficient wax or ineffective waxless pattern.
2. Too stiffly cambered skis for your technique or the snow conditions.
3. No weight shift onto your front ski.
4. Pushing back only with your kick. Try pressing down as well to make the wax grip.
5. Kicking late, behind your center of gravity. Try obtaining the major thrust with your legs when your feet are directly under your body.

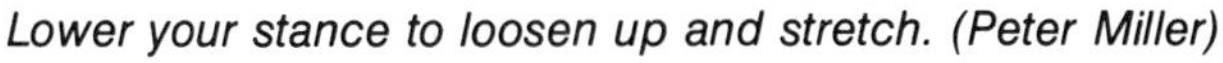
Lower your stance to loosen up and stretch. (Peter Miller)

Use your poles for setting your rhythm and pushing yourself forward. (Peter Miller)

Poling

Improve your kick and glide by working on your arms? Absolutely. Correct arm and poling motion is the key to better skiing. The manner in which you use your poles dictates your rhythm, body position, relaxation, speed.

Many beginners use their poles solely as outriggers or as canes for balance. Outriggers help you stay upright but supply no push down the track. Abandon the notion of poles as training wheels. You should be working your arms vigorously, depending on the grip of your wax and the incline of the trail, to supply a good deal of your forward power.

Plant your pole (stick it into the snow) in front so it is angled backward for immediate push. Push straight down and back past your hip. Your poling motion should take place half in front and half in back of your body when skiing on the flat, or you lose much of your pushing potential.

To recover the pole, bring it forward again at an angle, swinging your hand like a pendulum past your hip. Don't try to lift the pole vertically over the snow. This can lead to some pretty bizarre recovery motions, including the swim, the windmill, the roundhouse, the disposal of the dead mouse, and the pattycake. One thing they all have in common is lifting rather than swinging the pole forward.

Be definite both in recovering and planting the pole. A weak action here or a super-slow rhythm will allow your pole to skip along the snow as it is coming forward and throw you off balance and timing.

If pushing the poles past your hip seems awkward, you may be gripping them too tightly. Cradle the pole in your hand; hold it with a firm looseness. For maximum thrust with a relaxed arm, release your grip on the handle as you extend back. Some skiers let go of the pole completely, allowing it to hang from the strap. As an arm swings forward, the snug strap pulls the pole back into the hand. I prefer to release my pole only with my last three fingers. This gives me total extension, yet allows me to retain control of the pole action with my thumb and forefinger.

If your pole inexplicably seems to flap out of your grip, it may be because the handle lacks a knob at the top which fits between thumb and forefinger. If this is the case, you

For easy poling, release your grip on the pole as you push back. (Peter Miller)

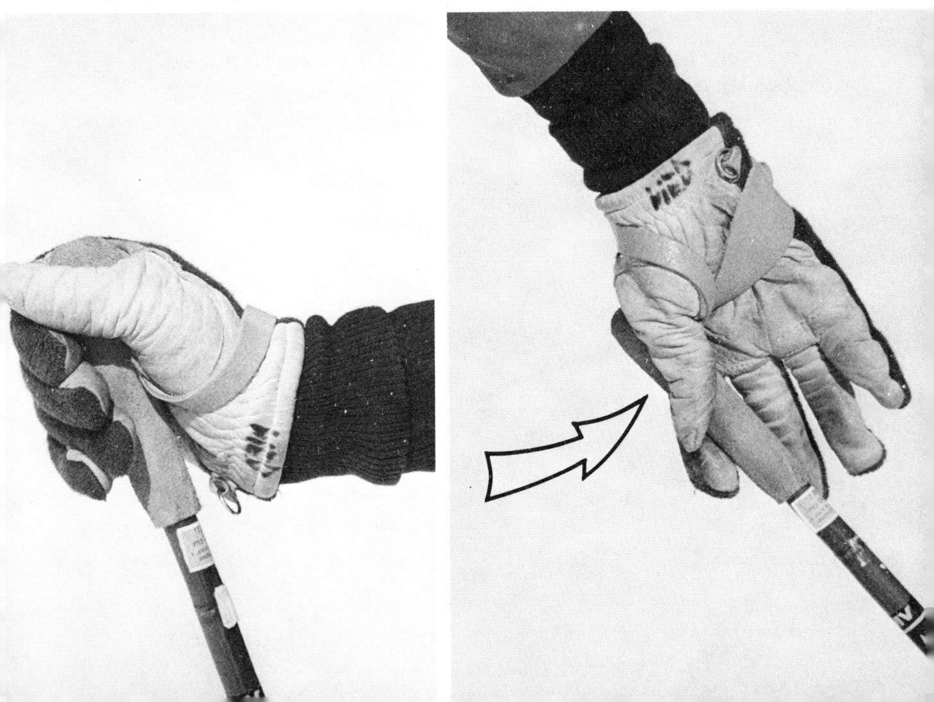

can make one by taping the top inch of the strap to the handle with several turns of electricians' tape.

For more power and efficiency, your arms should swing like pendulums from the shoulders when poling, as they do when you walk. Larger shoulder muscles provide more thrust than arm and elbow muscles. Shoulders that are locked force the arms to move only from the elbows, resulting in weak, choppy poling.

Comfortably bent arms provide a structure of maximum power for the energy expended. Think of how you would pull a tree over by tugging on a rope. Would you pull with straight arms or slightly bent?

If you're a slow-paced skier, you should keep your hands low in front: bring them up to belly level but no higher. Low hands provide maximum thrust at slow speeds. As you become a better skier carrying real speed down the track, your arms will lift higher, and you'll have a tremendous sensation of the tempo and forward recovery or swing of your arms setting your overall pace. Your whole body is drawn ahead by your arms coming through quickly. It's just like running: recall how much you work your arms when you want to move into a sprint.

Hands lifted too high in front bring your upper body back off your skis with each stride in a bobbing motion which directs much of your energy up into the air instead of down

WRONG! Incorrect use of the arms fouls up the rest of your technique. (Peter Miller)

Without using your legs, you cannot afford to be inefficient in your poling. (Peter Miller)

the trail. It also slows your tempo, provides only a push down into the snow instead of a push forward, and allows no push or extension of your poling behind your leg.

Worse yet is the habit many people develop of reaching too far forward with an absolutely straight arm. This will spread poison to the rest of your technique as it slows your tempo, lessens your power, gives you a sore back, prevents you from being forward on your gliding ski, stiffens your knees, fouls up your rhythm, and gives you a late kick, making you generally impotent on your skis. Now, will you ever again reach forward with a straight arm?

Try this exercise to get the feel of efficient poling. Find a slightly downhill track and push yourself along with your poles alone, in an alternating rhythm. Don't use your legs, but make sure you bend your knees slightly — it's easier. Working hard? That's how much energy you should use, even when striding. Experiment to discover what is most efficient. Straighten your arms, bend them, angle your poles differently, raise your hands high or low in front, grip your poles differently. You'll soon discover the most efficient means of propelling yourself. It doesn't take bulging muscles for this one, only correct technique. Once you feel it, you'll ski a new and easier way.

Double-Poling

One skiing maneuver uses arms only: double-poling, in which you use both poles together to push yourself along, thus giving your legs a rest. Use it whenever you want to keep up speed on fast flats or on gradual downhills. Beyond this, get a feeling for when double-poling works best by skiing with someone else. If the other person is striding, try double-poling and see which works best. Double-poling is also extremely stable because you are standing securely on both skis, which makes the technique useful where the trail is broken, chaotic, or icy.

When we skied across Alaska's Brooks Range in 1972, we came across a huge area of overflow ice. The Koyukuk River had frozen all the way to the bottom, damming itself and creating an ice skating rink measuring 2 miles by 3 miles. We had no alternative but to ski over the ice as we entered the "Gates of the Arctic." We had no metal edges on our skis. Solution? Double-poling for 3 miles. We still felt like dogs scampering about on a greased floor, and Jack

To double-pole, "fall" forward onto your poles, then push with your arms. (Peter Miller)

Miller once fell so hard that his aluminum pack frame bent. But it was the most stable technique we could use since we'd forgotten our ice skates!

Double-poling may look as if it is done totally with the arms, but most of the power is generated by the weight of your upper body compressing downward and pushing back on the ski poles. Your upper body "falling onto your poles" gives you a free ride with little muscle work.

Start by reaching forward with arms slightly bent at the elbows and planting your poles pointed slightly back. Bend at the waist, dropping forward and down on your poles. It is critical to keep your arms in a fixed position as you compress in order to transfer your upper body power to your poles. "Giving way" with your arms is inefficient. Only when you're bent over (with your upper body nearly parallel to the snow if you're a power skier) should you complete the double-pole by straightening your arms with a final push.

Double-poling is the only time in X-C skiing that you hinge at the waist, up and down. Pretend that you are

pumping an old-fashioned railroad handcar up and down as you move along the trail. The downward compression of the body onto the poles is done at the waist, not the knees. Your knees should be relaxed and flexed a bit but should not provide the dropping motion. This causes the most common error of double-poling ("sitting in a chair"), which puts your weight back, absorbing the force that should propel you down the track.

Kick double-pole: When it becomes too hard or too slow to maintain your speed, add a kick to your double-pole rhythm before you revert to your slower speed diagonal stride. This push down and back with one leg or the other will extend the speed range through which you can double-pole.

Adding a kick to your double-pole will provide more push at slower speeds. (Peter Miller)

WRONG! Don't "sit in a chair." (Peter Miller)

5

SKILLS FOR SKIING HILLS

UPHILL

For most Alpine skiers there is nothing sublime about climbing a hill (they've invented other means of dealing with vertical). Even cross-country skiers may find uphills tedious and troublesome. But covering great gulps of terrain, no matter uphill or down, is one of the pleasures of touring. With proper technique and equipment, skiing uphill can be an easy and graceful pleasure.

Most folks have to hike hills rather than cruise them because of a lack of confidence and aggressiveness. You need make only a few adjustments to your flat-track technique and have a willingness to raise your pulse rate a little to ski straight up most hills. The trick is to get a subtle feeling of where your weight is on your skis. Lean too far forward and your skis will slip because your center of gravity is in front of your feet; lean too far back and you will feel slow and awkward as if you are sitting in a chair and pulling yourself up the slope.

Try to be light on your feet and to feel the snow under your skis. Drop a little lower in your knees and body and shorten your stride, just as you would if you were running the hill on foot without skis. John Caldwell's description of going up hills in a "dog trot" is the best overall conceptualization I've heard. Jog up the hills as if you didn't have skis on — it's the thing you know best.

Arms usually supply lots of the power on the uphills, especially if your skis are waxed a bit too slippery. Keep your hands fairly low and your poles angled back so you can push effectively.

All your energy should be going forward up the hill. Many people I see on hills are bouncing up and down, half of their energy wasted into the air. Keep your head steady

Hills don't have to be difficult if you keep your weight over your feet and jog lightly up. (Peter Miller)

and your arms moving straight ahead, and your body will follow.

This technique will work for you regardless of the speed you choose to attack the hills: either walking or jogging.

You will achieve good grip on the snow as long as your weight is over your kicking foot. As your foot comes forward, "hit" the ski with your heel for just an instant. This is the easiest way to key in on correct weight position. If your heel can contact the ski, your weight must be directly over that foot. Then roll over the ball of your foot as you kick back and propel yourself forward.

Here is the classic predicament that many people work themselves into on a hill, guaranteeing a slip. (1) Poles are straight up and down, supplying no power. (2) Knees are straight so the heel cannot contact the ski for proper weight placement. (3) Body is way bent over at the waist,

WRONG! Don't make it hard on yourself. (Peter Miller)

putting the body's center of gravity far ahead of the feet. Simply looking up the hill will help put your weight properly on your skis. (For years native Vermonters have used the term "way bent over" to describe somebody who is extraordinarily stupid.)

Herringboning

When the hill becomes very steep or your wax starts to slip, it's time to break into a duck walk for extra grip.

Spread the tips of your skis far apart, keeping the tails together to form a wedge, or reverse snowplow. Tip your skis severely on their inside edges so they bite into the snow for hold. Bend your knees forward and inside. Step *forward* in this spread-eagle position in your regular ski striding rhythm. "Chop" little steps in the snow with each stride. If the herringbone feels awkward, you are probably waddling uphill with your weight too far back or stepping on the tail of the opposite ski.

When you start slipping, break into a herringbone for more climbing power. (Peter Miller)

Sidestepping

On super-steep inclines where you are hesitant about negotiating the terrain, sidestepping is the technique of last resort. It's slow and tedious, but wonderfully secure going both up and down.

Place your skis across the fall line and roll your ankles into the slope to edge your skis for grip. (The fall line is defined as the snowball's path of least resistance down the hill.) Step up or down by shifting your weight from one ski to the other. In deep snow, control your ski by lifting up with your toes and pressing down with your heel. On an icy slope, lean your body away from the slope for secure edge bite. Leaning into the hill will push your edges off the snow, often leading to a bruising slide.

Traversing

Often instead of sidestepping straight up or down, traversing (a zigzagging) on a gradual angle is an easier solution to a steep slope, especially when toting a heavy

Although it may look like it, you don't have to be a ballet dancer to change directions. (Peter Miller)

backpack. A clever route which tacks around the worst obstacles is extremely efficient in deep snow or on long mountain tours where energy must be conserved.

Kick Turn

How do you turn around at the end of each zig or zag? A kick turn will change your direction 180°. The quicker you do this little ballet maneuver, the better your chances are of success. Always turn facing downhill — you obviously cannot force your ski through the hill looming above you. Help your balance by planting your poles firmly behind you as you look downhill.

Kick (thus the name kick turn) your lower ski forward, then around in an arc so it faces the opposite direction. Now you are standing like Charlie Chaplin, feet protruding in either direction. To hesitate is to lose. Quickly shift weight onto the ski pointed in the new direction and bring the other one around parallel. I'd try this one on the flat the first few times, working up to steeper terrain.

DOWNHILL

Many skiers without downhill experience are surprised at the amount of downhill they have to deal with on cross-country skis. Some feel there is a conspiracy between gravity and a well-waxed ski: point the skis downhill and they seem to have a will of their own. But downhill skiing on cross-country skis both for novices and for more experienced skiers has only recently been getting the attention that it deserves. This is all the more important as downhill skiers add cross-country to their winter pleasures and as cross-country skiers ride the lifts with loose heels and head for steep back-country terrain on light equipment. Ski adventurer Allan Bard says, "The place you choose and the tools you use are up to you. It's all skiing." So many of the slopes that have traditionally been skied with heavy ski-mountaineering equipment are now being done with 3-pin equipment. It's not unusual anymore to see a knicker-clad figure on and among the moguls (humps and bumps of the slope), or to find cross-country skiers choosing heavier, metal-edged equipment to tackle steep, icy slopes without feeling like traitors to their sport.

All over the country skiers seem to be rediscovering the early days of Alpine skiing in the 1930s. Trapp instructors on a holiday often head off to the top of Mt. Mansfield, Vermont's highest peak, to ski the Teardrop, a magnificent if narrow Alpine trail cut in 1937 and since abandoned, available now to skiers who are willing to climb up in order to ski down, whatever their equipment. Not only are we using some of the old trails, but by looking at some of the photographs of skiers in the 1930s — their low, stable stance utilizing extreme edging — we get a good image of the technique that a cross-country skier needs for skiing down hills.

A word to Alpine skiers venturing onto skinny skis. Relative to Alpine equipment, cross-country gear is unforgiving on downhills. The skis are lighter, narrower, more flexible, and usually have no metal edges; boots are ordinarily only ankle-high, and heels lift freely off the skis. This means less control and stability than available on Alpine equipment, leading many Alpine skiers to charge that "these skis can't be turned, they have no edges." No

Endless telemarks in Garibaldi Provincial Park. (David Knudson)

steel edges, perhaps, but after all the bottom is not round (there's a right angle where sidewall meets bottom) and you still keep the curved end in front. We've found that the problem is not so much equipment as misinformation and superstition. One expert Alpine skier in a cross-country class protested that she couldn't do parallel turns on cross-country skis. Had she ever tried? No, but she'd often been told that they couldn't be done. Her instructor urged her to give them a try. The result, not surprisingly, was a dozen short-swing parallel turns and on-going bliss. Other Alpine skiers may not have such immediate results, but they'll find they'll ski pretty much the same way on both kinds of equipment, with some subtle differences.

Modern downhill equipment permits some Alpine skiers to turn by banking (leaning their bodies into the hill), with less edging, more skidding, and less emphasis on the position of the hands. Metal edges are so sharp and boots so stiff that it is not necessary to edge radically in order for the ski to hold and carve a turn. Since your heel is firmly attached to the ski, with Alpine bindings you can press forward and down on the top of your ski to initiate the turn with the ski tip. Loose-heeled X-C equipment allows you to press *around* a turn, but not forward and down. Further, the tip of a cross-country ski is more flexible, so you really do not carve a turn on it as with an Alpine ski, you turn more on the mid-body of the ski.

If you are a really good Alpine skier or racer, then everything you do in Alpine has direct carry-over into X-C downhill skiing because you are used to edging and unweighting (see page 76) radically in turns, keeping your hands low and in front, and getting the most out of your equipment.

But if you are an intermediate or novice Alpine skier and are used to turning by banking or swiveling, you will have to make some adjustments to be competent on skinny skis — nothing radical, a little more edging and a little more unweighting.

To compensate for the light equipment, your weight must be right over the centers of your skis or you'll be on your rear end. To repeat: it's not easy to balance on a narrow, sliding platform, especially when you are basically wearing a soft running shoe attached to the ski only at the tip of the toe!

Skiing downhill on X-C skis is good practice for Alpine skiers. No longer can you "cheat" while turning and get away with it because of the stable holding power of Alpine equipment. Downhill X-C will bring you back to basics. You'll learn a tremendous amount about balance, weight, steering, and edging which is directly applicable to Alpine.

Keep your knees bent and your hands low and in front for stability. (Peter Miller)

Body Position

Ski downhill in the same ready but relaxed position you would use to receive a tennis serve, with your weight over your feet at all times to maintain better control of your skis and ski much longer without getting tired. (Avoid "sitting" with your rear or bending forward at your waist.) Notice in the photo above that my ankles are bent and pressed forward against the top lace of my boot. This is of utmost importance because it causes the knees to flex forward as well. Flexed knees act as shock absorbers and make steering possible. As German-born instructor Adi Yoerg says, "You cannot ski with knees like the goat."

Though you flex your knees properly, if your hands are in the air (victim of an Alpine hold-up?) you'll be hard-pressed to make a turn or be very secure on a straight downhill run. Few skiers realize the importance of hand position. Your body will follow your hands. I like to keep my hands low and in front as if they are gripping bicycle handlebars. This will keep the body forward, square, and facing in the direction of the turn. Ski with your hands where you can use them easily. Hands that are too high or too far back (i.e., out of your field of vision) will throw you off balance.

Straight Run

Letting your skis run straight down the fall line of a slope to a natural stop as the slope flattens is a good way to get used to a bit of speed. Keep your skis hip-width apart for stability and good balance and your poles angled backward to avoid catching the stray bush or skier. Begin on a slope that is comfortable for you, getting acquainted with all the slight adjustments you'll have to make for bumps and ripples in the snow. This, by the way, is not just an exercise for the rankest beginner but something you'll return to often in your skiing as you find downhill slopes on which you can simply let your skis run. Often it is more secure to run straight with more speed than you might like than to try to pull out by turning.

Later on as you begin skiing trails, try getting all you can out of each straight downhill. You'll be amazed how much speed you can carry onto the flats. Racers occasionally attain speeds of 30-35 mph, but be assured that they know the runout is safe. This is all free distance covered, normal breathing restored. Try tucking (crouching) for

To get up, simply roll over and forward onto your knees, then stand. (Peter Miller)

more speed. If your legs are fatigued, rest by keeping your legs straight and lean over in your upper body only.

Getting Up After

When things go amiss in downhill skiing, it's usually in a delightfully big way with terrific explosions of snow. The best laughs I've had while skiing are during the disentangling operation after a fall. Unless you fall, you aren't trying anything new. But unless you're endowed with Neanderthal arms, you need a bit of technique to hoist yourself upright without getting uptight in the battle with gravity.

To get up from a fall, roll over onto your side so your skis are parallel, downhill from you, and across the fall line of the slope so they will not slide forward or back. If you are submerged in deep snow, forming an X with your poles will provide a stable platform to push off. Then simply move forward onto your knees. Your weight is now over your knees. Rock back onto your feet and stand up. No thrashing necessary!

Edge Sense

Stopping or turning on your cross-country skis will be a lot easier if you've come to an understanding with the edges of your skis. Here are a few ways to make their acquaintance.

1. Stand stationary across the hill. Roll your ankles into the slope to edge your skis. Try to push your downhill ski outward (downward). It won't move if it is edged. Now flatten your downhill ski on the snow and push it outward. It will skid easily (sideslip).

2. Stand across a groomed slope. Flatten both skis and sideslip down the hill. Roll your ankles and knees into the hill to edge your skis and stop. Repeat the flattening and edging several times.

Snowplow Stop

Newly sensitive to the edging of the skis, you're ready to develop some resources for stopping, unless you prefer

Get a feel for your edges before heading downhill. (Peter Miller)

A super-wide snowplow will provide stability and maximum edging. (Peter Miller)

your descents quick and free of control. The place to begin is with a snowplow, so called because you're plowing snow.

With your knees and hands properly positioned, let your skis run downhill, then spread them apart equally into a wedge position by pressing the tails out *flat* with your heels, keeping the ski tips together. Once the tails of the skis are spread apart, rolling your ankles inward will set the skis on their inside edges, digging in sufficiently for braking. If skis are over-edged they may cross; if they are too flat they will not brake.

The wider the wedge and the more you edge, the slower you'll go. Keep the pressure on and you'll come to a gradual stop, regrettably not on the proverbial dime. (One thing I've found is that the snowplow is oversold as a means to

It is easier to start with half-plows. (Peter Miller)

put the brakes on firmly in a radical downhill. To do that you'll have to turn up into the hill—but more on that later.)

The wider apart you hold your knees, the more effective your snowplow will be. Knock-knees aren't effective: bend your knees forward, not together, and keep them far enough apart to hold a beachball between them.

A super exercise for learning the feeling of edging a ski in a snowplow is to traverse a groomed slope at an easy angle. With much of your weight on your uphill ski, push your downhill ski out into a half plow. Edge the ski to the inside to slow your speed and stop.

Another great exercise for getting the feel for initiating a snowplow stop is what I call the "straight and spread routine." Head straight down a gentle slope with your skis parallel. Before gaining much speed, spread and sink into a definite snowplow. But don't stop completely! Just before you lose momentum, draw your skis back parallel, gain speed, snowplow again, parallel, snowplow, etc. Try this on a slope long enough to allow a sequence of several near-stops.

Many people produce only a lopsided snowplow. Look at your tracks in the snow: both skis should be skidding, leaving a wake rather than a line. If not, correct by bringing *both* hips square to the direction you are heading so that your skis are equally weighted. Letting one hip fall back straightens that knee, makes you crooked on your skis, and leaves you with only a half-effective braking force. Keeping your hands square and in front is a good device for squaring your hips.

WRONG! Avoid the lopsided chicken wing! (Peter Miller)

Snowplow Turn

The snowplow turn is the turn of first resort, easily initiated by putting more pressure on one ski. It is extremely stable and the foundation for more advanced turns.

To learn a snowplow turn, head downhill in your regular sliding snowplow. As you press your skis out, shift your weight and stand on the outside ski that is pointed in the direction you want to go. (Thus, in the lefthand turn shown in the photo, my weight is on the right ski.) Lean to the outside of the turn as if centrifugal force were throwing you to the outside. As you put weight on this outside ski by applying heel pressure, edge it so it will hold on the snow. Steer around with your knees, always turning in the direction of the stronger ski. Lean right to turn left, like pushing a tiller away from you in a boat. Think of swooping down into a turn with your outside hand.

It's not uncommon to see a skier hurtling downhill while protesting loudly that the skis won't turn. The skier is usually standing upright on the skis and, instead of sinking in the knees to shift weight, is leaning with shoulders and head only, trying to nudge the skis around.

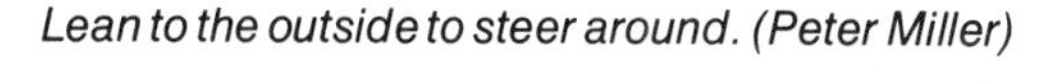

Lean to the outside to steer around. (Peter Miller)

Push-button snowplow: Here's Allan Bard's favorite way to teach a snowplow turn. While moving downhill in your regular wedge, imagine buttons underneath your heels. You will use these buttons to steer. To initiate a turn, push the "turning button" with your heel on the ski that's pointed in the direction you want to go (e.g., the right ski in the preceding photos).

If you're having trouble with the turn, put your hands on your bent knees. (This also puts you in the proper body position.) When you want to turn, simply press in on your outside or downhill knee with your hand. Push left knee in to go right, push right knee in to go left. Feel the rhythm. Pushing in on the downhill knee helps turning in three critical ways: (1) steers the downhill knee in the direction you want to turn; (2) places your weight on the downhill ski; (3) edges your downhill ski so it will carve around.

Work from a traverse: If you are still having difficulty getting the feel for it, traverse a slope and try a partial snowplow turn up into the hill using gravity to help you stop. This is less scary and more controlled than starting by going straight downhill. Progress by doing more distinct turns from a steeper traverse.

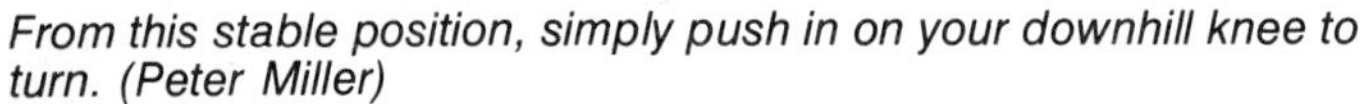

From this stable position, simply push in on your downhill knee to turn. (Peter Miller)

Step to stop: Here's where you can make a snowplow turn that will really stop you on a dime in case you're hurtling downhill and come upon a skier fallen in front of you. Make a very sharp, emphatic snowplow turn up into the side of the trail and step the uphill ski over next to the downhill steering ski with a motion like your old high school two-step dance. This is really a natural finish to a snowplow turn and is the gateway to parallel skiing, giving you a feeling of completing turns with maximum control.

Linking Your Turns

Turns downhill are actually easier when more than one is done so that the ending of one turn sets you up for the next, establishing a rhythm and cadence which blends the individual ingredients of turning into one flowing motion. Once you learn the ABC's of doing a snowplow, skate, stem christie, parallel, or telemark turn, try to link several

Snowplow turns can be linked even in deep snow. (Peter Miller)

together. This is what skiing is really about: negotiating the slope as if all your turns were tied to each other. "She can really crank her skis right and left" is truly a complimentary way of saying someone is a good skier.

Stepping and Skating Turns

The most obvious way to turn on cross-country skis is simply to pick one up, point in the direction you want to go, and bring the other one over next to it, in what is commonly called a step turn. It will feel a lot less awkward if you try to pick up and turn the tip of the ski rather than get the whole thing around. At first you'll feel somewhat defensive, barely able to get the skis around in time. Soon you'll be scampering, stepping quickly into or out of the tracks and around the looming trees. At this point you might get a little more aggressive and indulge in accelerating skating turns, already familiar to Alpine skiers and skaters on blades and wheels.

Stepping or skating is often the only type of turn you can do when you are locked into deep-set machine tracks or dealing with tricky snow that catches tails and edges of skis. It is also a very fast turn in which little speed is lost. A single skate turn will accomplish a minimal change of direction; several skates in succession will cover a larger radius. I use skate turns to negotiate corners on the flat when my speed is fairly fast, and on downhills when my speed is not so fast that I must make a parallel carved turn.

To make a skate turn, keep your knees flexed and poles out for balance (photo A). You must edge your outside ski to give yourself a secure nonslip platform from which to step (B). The critical ingredient is the weight shift from the outside ski to the inside ski (C). This takes a real commitment to throw your weight into the turn and to the inside. You must be able to stand on one ski, then the other, and do it quickly.

The skate turn is not only useful in itself but is also the best way I know to learn to edge your skis for bite in the snow. It is a great exercise for getting the feeling of the usefulness of bent knees in turning, and the feeling of transferring weight from one ski to the other — both critical elements in performing more advanced turns.

Shift weight to step around.
(Peter Miller)

Now bring your ski parallel after your snowplow turn. (Peter Miller)

Stem Christie

The stem christie is a faster, more definite and prettier turn than a snowplow. Begin with your skis parallel and traverse the hill at a 45° angle. Push or step out with the unweighted uphill ski to form a wedge. Thus in starting the righthand turn shown here my left ski is pushed out (A). Complete this snowplow part of the turn two-thirds of the way around. Now bring your skis parallel by gradually shifting or stepping your weight completely over to the outside (downhill) ski so that the inside ski comes in effortlessly. In this position, traverse the hill parallel in preparation for the next turn. By bringing your skis parallel at the end of the turn you learn to pick up one ski and float it so that you're not always on both skis as you are in the snowplow.

For your first stem-christie turns, snowplow across the fall line, then close your skis, bringing them parallel. Gradually reduce the snowplow part of the turn so you bring your skis parallel earlier and move toward parallel skiing.

Parallel Turns

You don't necessarily have to do parallel turns to be a competent skier on cross-country skis. But if you're comfortable with stem christies, parallel turns are only a short slide away and will give you more control through a faster, tighter turn. Despite what you may have heard, you do not have to be an Alpine skier to learn to ski parallel. We've often seen beginning skiers at Trapp's produce a parallel turn instead of the intended stem christie or, rarely, snowplow turns. Here's how:

Work from a platform: In linked parallel turns, speed is checked by setting the edges at the completion of each turn. This is done by a sharp pushing of the heels down into the snow and an acute flexing of the knees forward and sideways into the hill (A). This sharp interruption of your momentum from your edge set creates a rebound which makes unweighting for the next turn easier. At the same time, a hard pole plant and forward thrust with the downhill pole also helps this rebound. Sink your knees and plant your poles to trigger the turn.

Weight: For your knees to do the job, you'll need an assist from properly placed body weight. To keep weight on your downhill ski you'll have to lean out and over it, that is, away from, not into, the hill even while your knees are driving into the hill. In this way you avoid banking your turns like a water skier — a habit which usually leads to falls on X-C skis.

Unweighting: To get my weight off both skis, I spring up and forward (B) to release the edge and free my skis in order to steer them around. Now that my skis are unweighted, a change of direction is possible and the skis will run to the fall line.

Change direction: Photo C shows me pressing forward and down on my skis with my knees steering in the new direction. This pressure down and forward controls the tips of the skis. The harder the pressure, the sharper the turn. Notice the change in the ski edges as I come around the turn, the push downward with the heels, and my outside hand driving in the direction of the turn. My knees are bent, especially the outside one, and my weight has been transferred mostly to the downhill ski. To edge, I'm point-

A

B

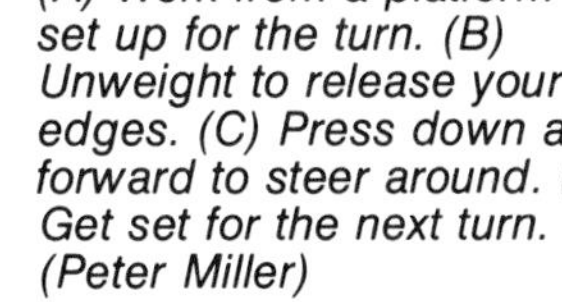

(A) Work from a platform to set up for the turn. (B) Unweight to release your edges. (C) Press down and forward to steer around. (D) Get set for the next turn. (Peter Miller)

C

D

ing my knees to the inside of the turn.

Photo D shows both the finish of the turn and the set position for the next turn.

Poling: At this point in the anatomy lesson one should pause to find out a little more about hands and poles. The hands are really beginning the turn. You are essentially turning around your downhill pole, and planting it decisively is a way of saying "get ready" to turn your skis. It helps you make up your mind which way to go. Once that pole is in, go that way. Reaching out with your hand keeps your body forward and over your skis, ready to initiate the turn. Keep driving that hand forward throughout the turn, or you will ski past your pole, twisting your body back and out of position and reducing the bite of your edges on the snow. If you're having a hard time getting from one turn to the other, check your hands.

While your downhill hand is planting the pole, what is your other hand doing? If it is lazy and has drifted back past your hip, it will be hard to bring the skis around for your next turn. No matter which hand is planting the pole, they should both be out to the side and in front (within your field of vision) as if you were embracing an enormous snowman or holding the handlebars of a grossly oversized bicycle so that you'll be square on your skis for easier and quicker turns.

John Dostal, who had the distinction of learning to Alpine ski after years of cross-country, observes that "there is a functional difference in using long X-C poles for doing Alpine-style turns. The shorter Alpine poles, planted vertically, bring you forward onto your skis. Plant a X-C pole vertically and your hand will be so high that your weight will be thrown back off your skis. If you are doing only lift-served skiing on your sticks, use a shorter pole (but don't expect as much out of your diagonal stride or double-poling as you're heading for the lift). When using a normal X-C-length pole you must re-create the short pole feeling. You'll probably find that you have to cock your wrist, getting the hand forward and the basket way out in front of the pole plant."

Rhythm: Maintaining your rhythm is essential when making linked parallel turns. Allow one turn to lead into the next, making you feel as if you're "bouncing" from left

Rhythm makes one turn into an enjoyable series near Early Winter Spire in the North Cascades. (David Knudson)

A

B

Hockey stop: This will get you to turn your skis quickly. (Peter Miller)

to right as you turn down the slope. Your decisive yet smooth pole plant sets your rhythm. Remember to keep your upper body quiet and facing mostly downhill throughout the turns, and look ahead far enough so you can set your moves and timing. If your head doesn't swivel, your body won't, either. For a little help here, station a friend downhill and keep your eyes on him or her as you make your turns.

Exercises for learning parallel turns: *"Breaking your tails loose"*: To get the feeling of starting a turn with your skis together, traverse a slope, sink, and as you start to rise up, turn up into the hill by pushing the tails of your skis down the hill, or breaking them loose. Try this from progressively steeper traverses and with more speed.

"Hockey stop": Here you're breaking the tails loose more emphatically, carrying a little more speed as you ski down the fall line. The photo sequence shows me (A) "crouching" or unweighting my skis, (B) rising up to unweight the skis, and (C) quickly turning my skis across the fall line in a skidding stop just as I'd stop on hockey skates. My skis are

C

Snowplow short swing: This helps you loosen up your knees and feel the rhythm of linked turns. (Peter Miller)

skidding sideways and I'm biting into the snow as hard as I can with my edges to stop crisply. The hockey stop also works effectively as an emergency stop when someone skis in front of you unexpectedly or you discover that a stream has cut across the trail during late spring skiing.

"Snowplow short swing": This exercise develops the rhythm of linked turns and is the best connector of turns that I have yet found. It forces you to flex your knees to steer your skis. If you can do this one, I guarantee you can do parallel turns!

Head straight down a gentle slope in a *shallow* snowplow, and from this narrow wedge do quick and continuously linked turns. As soon as your weight comes onto one ski and you start to turn, get off that ski and onto the other and turn in that direction. Think of it as making decisive half turns. This teaches rhythm, edge change, weight shift, some rebounding, steering in the knees, and a pole plant. As you master this, progressively bring the skis together more and move into parallel skiing.

Imitation is an excellent teacher here. Follow another skier closely and stay in his tracks so you imitate and feel the rhythm and bounce.

Stay low and forward when bombing. (Peter Miller)

Speeding without Spilling

Even the most competent ski swivelers get into situations where turns will not be the order of the day. The time will come when you simply have to ride it out. High speeds don't necessarily have to be terrifying (indeed they may become addictive).

If you want to hang on in high speed bombing, hands should be positioned low and in front to maintain a lower body position (like an opened up tuck), ankles and knees flexed for steerage and to act as shock absorbers, feet apart for stability, and weight directly over your skis. It's as if you're rising up slightly out of the downhill racer's tuck, extending your hands forward and to the side. If you're hurtling through a sweeping corner, stay in this position and steer with your hands, driving the outside hand in the direction of the turn. To get a feeling for the hand drive and weight shift, try it when you're stationary on the flat. Drive your left arm and hand forward and feel the weight come onto your left leg and ski. At high speeds this will pull you around a right turn as long as you stay low, keeping your arm out front as well as down. Dragging your poles, especially the inside one, like outriggers will give more stability, but be careful not to snag baskets on a branch or root.

Flying Buttocks Arrest
("Parallel bun stop" for more advanced skiers)

In the event of failure to stay on your skis while attempting to execute any kind of turn or schuss on the trail, you must learn to make a proper sitzmark, demonstrated in the photo. Points awarded for burying the head, for flagrant travel over the tips of the skis, securing maximum air time, devastation of equipment, shrub and tree pruning and removal.

The Master demonstrates a flying buttocks arrest. (Peter Miller)

Telemark turns in deep powder. (Peter Miller)

Telemark Turns

It is not uncommon to ride the lifts at a downhill resort these days and hear fellow riders calling to that lone cross-country skier venturing onto the slopes, "Telemark!" What they're asking for is a turn that's been around ever since skis were 12 feet long and attached to feet by reindeer thongs. It's a satisfying, flamboyant turn and the only one you can't also do with Alpine skis. This is the one turn that makes the most of a loose heel. Recently we've seen a revival of the telemark as X-C skiers and mountaineers alike rediscover the challenge, usefulness, and just plain fun of sweeping downhill leaving a single carved track. If you're in rough snow and find it difficult to turn two skis at once, drop into a telemark, essentially putting yourself on one long ski. No wonder ski jumpers land in a telemark position.

When I link a series of telemarks down a slope of unbroken powder I feel like a huge hawk soaring on the wind

currents. But the telemark is not just another pretty turn from the history of skiing. Occasionally I'll run into a snow condition which makes it impossible to turn my X-C skis in a parallel stance, like settled powder snow which is fairly dense. Here a telemark is in its element. It provides the steering power that is needed to plow through the awkward snow.

How to learn to do it?

From a diagonal stride: This may be the easiest way to learn how to telemark. As you move down a gentle slope, simply extend your legs as if you were diagonal striding, then steer around with your front knee in the direction you wish to go. Notice how the tip of the rear ski will nestle into the instep of your forward foot. In other words, do a split, then turn! Many skiers don't realize how low you have to sink. They would do well to make several traverses of gentle slopes, sinking onto alternate forward knees before giving any thought to turning.

From a snowplow: A telemark turn is really only an exaggerated snowplow turn with one ski following the other in the same track. Another way of getting the feel of telemarking is by using the familiar plow as a starting position.

The first photo shows me starting an ordinary snowplow turn on a groomed slope. In the second photo I have started to do a kind of split and put much of my weight on my forward leg. I've let my other ski float back, which actually happens automatically as soon as I bend my front knee more. I'm now in half a telemark position, and as the rear ski continues to float, it becomes relatively parallel (with its tail flared out a bit) but well behind in full telemark.

To turn, I'm using the same steering force in my telemark position as I use in my old snowplow turn. My downhill knee is weighted, bent forward, and pointed to the inside of the turn in the direction I want to go. My ski is edged to hold on the snow and carve around. My snowplow turn has shifted into a reasonably good telemark.

Work from your familiar snowplow to ease into a telemark. (Peter Miller)

 Steer with your front ski, carve with your rear ski. (Peter Miller)

Turning power: The tremendous *steering power* in a telemark turn is obtained from a drastically bent forward knee. At the beginning of the turn, drop down onto your forward knee. Genuflect. The more you emphasize your weight dropping onto your forward ski, the more specific the turn will be. Drive your knee and hip into and around the turn. When I pull off a good telemark turn, I feel as if my whole body is merely following the direction my forward knee is steering.

The *carving power* of a telemark is, to a large extent, from the rear ski. More difficult snow and terrain require more weight on the rear ski and feet closer together. I call this a half telemark. Using the rear ski is the key to making the telemark more useful than pretty and taking it away from the packed easy slopes. Most people neglect the rear ski. When the going gets tough, I revert to my half telemark and use my rear ski to help edge, carve, steer, and stabilize my turns.

As in every other skiing endeavor, you must adapt to the conditions and terrain. You can execute telemark turns pretty much totally on your front ski on groomed slopes; but your rear ski is used more and your feet are closer together as the skiing becomes more tricky. By doing a less radical split your weight is more evenly distributed between your two skis, so if one ski catches you can correct on the other.

While learning a telemark, most folks get the feel of their front ski turning, but then the rear ski "washes out" or skitters downhill and control is lost. It is difficult to say how much weight you should have on your back ski, to give you a percentage. You simply need enough to finish the turn and still be carving a nice thin track in the snow. Look at it this way: how much weight can you put on your rear ski if the heel of your boot is up off the ski?

In the fore and aft telemark position, some lateral stability is vital. Keep your arms up and out to the side, using them as outriggers. On a shaky telemark a quick touch of pole to snow will put you back in balance.

Sink and link: Now try several turns together. The rhythm of linked turns is essential for learning the telemark well. One turn should lead into the next. To initiate each turn, drop down onto your front ski with a scissorlike action of your legs. Push your knee forward as well as down. Drive forward with your hands. Rise up on the toe of your rear ski. Put more or less weight on the rear ski according to the difficulty of the terrain and snow conditions. When you come around, rise up, switch feet, and sink down into the next turn. In linked turns, you apply more weight on your rear ski as your feet change leads. You'll rapidly feel the scissoring rhythm.

In 1977 we skied nearly 500 miles around the northern tip of Ellesmere Island, along with Greenland the northernmost land in the world. After leaving the sea pack ice, we hauled our heavy one-man sleds up to the top of the Grand Land Ice Cap. Hard work, but a new experience waited on the other side. Before us lay miles of gently sloping glacial fields covered with light new snow, clearly an opportunity for an orgy of telemarking. Nobody had yet telemarked with a 200-pound sled strapped behind, but the sleds had to go down the slope too. So off we pushed, linking the prettiest telemarks imaginable, the sleds well behaved but nudging us urgently. It was one of the high points in 52 days of continuous skiing: an old turn used in a new way in a new land.

An old turn used in a new way up near the North Pole. (Ned Gillette)

Ruth Glacier on Mt. McKinley. (Ned Gillette)

6
HANDLING TERRAIN

Skiing smoothly over varied terrain is one of cross-country skiing's really sensual pleasures, a way of getting clear of gravity and using it to your advantage. It's instinctive skiing on the trail that we all strive for, and it comes only with experience. The kind of refinements that allow you to ski successfully through any kind of terrain and snow condition don't lend themselves easily to textbook analysis. For example, I can't tell you when to stem into a downhill turn and when to step out of it, but only that the two can be combined as terrain dictates. The best I can do is to suggest some possibilities of dealing with terrain, leaving the refinements to your growing skills. They'll come quickly if you're willing to go back over a section of trail that may literally have thrown you, and if you stay alert to tracks left by preceding skiers. Have they skated around a turn or skidded? On uphills, have they herringboned or tackled the grade straight up?

One thing for certain: you'll want to be looking well ahead as you're skiing. With your eyes glued resolutely to your skis, you'll never be at a loss for how to spell Rossignol (or the brand of your choice), but you'll find the trail full of unsettling surprises rather than opportunities for smooth skiing.

Bumps

It is not uncommon to find bumpy, undulating flat and uphill sections of trail, especially early in the season when snow cover is sparse in the woods. The question is, How do you ski smoothly through these bumps when only part of your ski is touching the snow? Let your ski ride up the bump, then kick off the backside, suing it like a sprinter's block so you get an extra burst of speed and keep up your momentum. The precise timing of a hurdler is what you are after. To hit a bump just right for maximum push, you

Go for it! (Peter Miller)

must look ahead and be constantly adjusting the length of your stride so that you push just after your foot goes over the crest, perhaps taking an extra-long stride or a delicate half-stride at times.

Some bumps may be big enough so you'll want to break up your diagonal striding routine with one or two double-poles off the top, thus carrying more speed off the downhill. An experienced skier makes sure to double-pole off the downside of the bump, using gravity to the greatest advantage.

Once over a bump you may find yourself in a dip. Try to get through without imitating a suspension bridge, which will result in a decided lack of kick and glide and possibly a broken ski. To negotiate dips of less than a ski length, I slide one ski tip into the bottom of the hollow. Then, in one long stride, I shoot the other ski across to the other side of the dip. This gives me the two advantages I'm looking for: (1) no bridging; (2) a solid kick forward off the slope of the dip (sprinter's block). To negotiate dips of greater width, simply double-pole through, making sure your knees are flexed and weight is over your feet.

A moderately rolling downhill section well endowed with bumps gives an amusement park air to cross-country skiing. If you are just getting acquainted with skiing, soak up the bumps with your legs while keeping your upper body quiet. As you "hit" the bump, be ready to be pitched forward: compensate by flexing your legs and leaning back just a bit. Bumpy trails may give rollercoaster thrills but are not always rollercoaster smooth, so you may find one knee near your chest while the other is almost straight. So use independent leg action as an auto uses independent shock absorbers to smooth out the ride on a rough road, allowing you to make tiny adjustments to keep your skis on the snow.

If you don't soak up the bump, it will send you into the air, a condition often sught by more experienced and playful skiers who have checked the guarantee on their skis. While you are airborne, you'll want to remain relaxed and keep your weight over your skis, lowering your legs for landing and to absorb the shock of impact. We used to jump on cross-country skis on the 20-meter hill during my high school days. It was a gas, but a great depleter of team equipment!

Finally, bumps can be a natural aid to turning. Use the top of the bump as a pivot point around which to swivel your skis, sliding off the backside.

Extreme Downhills

Just because you are at the top of an intimidatingly steep slope or headwall, don't lose your cool. Even as a novice you already have all the technical moves necessary to descend fairly steep slopes. The width of the pitch will determine what you can get away with. Wide-open western slopes lend themselves to long traverses linked by kick turns or sidestepping. Take the slow and easy approach by seeking out the path of least resistance and utilizing these familiar techniques.

Whether you are turning or traversing on steep terrain, it is vital to lean out from the hill so your weight is over your feet while you drive your knees into the hill so your

Hanging on in steep, icy conditions. (Ned Gillette)

ski edges will grip. You can get a good feeling for this maneuver while still on the flat. Stand on your skis, extend one arm to the side, and have a friend tug steadily, trying to pull you off balance. You'll put up maximum resistance by driving your knees away from the pull. Look down and notice that your upper body is over your feet and that your skis are automatically on their edges. This may feel scary on a steep slope as you are poised looking down a breathtaking pitch, but your driving knees and edged skis will give you a reassuring platform. I at last completely understood this feeling of leaning away from what seems secure when I was traversing steep icy slopes in the Sierra, carrying a heavy backpack. Unless I consciously forced myself to lean far away from the slope, my mountaineering skis with climbing skins attached would begin to slip, which might have led to a dangerous fall as we crossed above a line of cliffs.

If you are unsure of changing directions by snowplow or parallel turn, remember "old trusty": the kick turn. This is the easiest way to link your traverses. When you want to slow down at the end of your traverse, simply point your skis up into the hill and stop, or use the half snowplow. Set yourself securely on the snow, and do kick around as quickly as possible. You don't want to hesitate while standing with one ski up in the air, precariously perched. Steep terrain demands that the lower ski should be kicked around first, turning away from the hill.

Remember that you don't have to go straight down, make turns, or even go across that steep slope. Sidestepping and slipping are super secure because you are using the full lengths of your ski edges to grip the snow. You can stand stationary as long as you wish and descend at your discretion. Use the same body position as for traversing.

Steep chutes can present grave problems, especially in the tree-shrouded East. They are usually narrow, and frequently packed hard by previous skiers, and very fast. It is often difficult to check your speed. If there is a good runout, you can usually let your skis run straight down a chute, but otherwise expect a prolonged session of snowplowing, which can be very tiring and difficult if the trail is not wide enough to allow you to plow with both skis. The solution is

Stay low and wide in steep chutes. (Ned Gillette)

to let one ski drift out in front and plow harder with that leg while resting the other one or keeping it clear of brush.

Wider chutes give more opportunities to control your speed. Use the terrain to your advantage by skiing up into the sides of the trail, turning, and heading back down and across to the other side to check speed. If you carry enough speed and remain relaxed and square over your skis with your hands out in front, you will find that the walls of the gully will nearly make the turn for you as you bank off their sides.

Ride the sides to check speed. (Peter Miller)

Extreme Uphills

Going up steep slopes can be as tedious as downhill can be thrilling. Look at the slope carefully, trying to pick out the most logical route around obstacles. Instead of butting heads with the hill straight on, consider traversing back and forth on a manageable angle, especially if you're breaking trail in deep snow or carrying a heavy backpack. If you have to sidestep, modify your technique so you step up and forward each time — much easier than scuttling sideways up the hill.

Whether you use light cross-country or heavier Alpine-like ski-mountaineering gear, give serious consideration to the use of climbing skins if you face long uphill climbs of hundreds of vertical feet. These pieces of artificial sealskin give foolproof grip up even the sharpest inclines. Commercially available skins are designed to fit on skis of Alpine proportions, but it is possible to cut your own thin strips of about 18 inches in length and tape them under the midsection of cross-country skis. My experience is that you must be extraordinarily careful when traversing steep, icy slopes because the thickness of the skin and hairs tend to lift the edge of the ski off the snow, possibly leading to a dangerous slide. At the top of the climb, simply remove the skins and head off downhill. (Another way to improvise climbers is to weave small-diameter rope over and under the length of the ski, in effect putting "chains" on your skis.)

Skier's Self-Arrest

On two occasions I've seen skiers resort to a ski pole self-arrest in life-threatening situations. (1) Doug Wiens halted a long slide on the icy headwall of a cirque on Ellesmere Island — he was using 3-pin boots and bindings. (2) On our first attempt to climb Mt. McKinley in a day, Galen Rowell slowed our fall enough to allow me to grab a fixed rope and stop us. His lightning-quick reactions gave him the opportunity to jam the ski pole tip into the snow up to the basket while gripping the pole at its base. This technique will probably stop you when nothing else will.

Also available for skiing in extreme conditions are specially designed ski poles with a plastic ice-axe-like spike protruding from the handle. (Don't be hesitant to change to climbing boots and crampons if you feel insecure on steep, icy terrain.)

Transitions

Skiing off a steep slope onto the flat tends to pitch you forward. To guard against this, sit back just a bit as you encounter the transition and be ready to soak up the deceleration with your legs. Better yet, don't take it straight on, but ski diagonally onto the flat. The most dramatic form of a transition is that which ski jumpers encounter on landing and, like them, you might want to use the telemark position for maximum fore-and-aft stability.

Tracks

In machine-set tracks, you won't have much opportunity to stop unless you lift one ski outside of the track and form a half snowplow. The trick is to not put the brakes on too quickly. Many beginners will simply jam a ski out into the snow and find themselves pitched forward by the abrupt deceleration. It is better to keep more of your weight over the ski that is still in the track and ease onto your braking and plowing ski, increasing the amount of edge and pressure to bring yourself to a stop. (I also use this half plow to slow my speed on sidehill traverses by standing on the uphill ski that is going straight and plowing with the lower ski, a secure maneuver in troublesome terrain and awkward snow.)

Aging tracks heavily traveled by skiers can turn from aids to obstacles. Sometimes it's the railroad switchyard effect as one track blends into the other for a few feet. Look ahead and plan for this. Nimble skiing is at a premium here. Get off the ski that is headed for trouble so that it will float as the other ski carries you through the distinct channel. Sometimes both tracks disappear, and here you stand securely on both skis, double-poling rather than diagonal-striding. If it is a really slippery section, put both skis on their inside edges for added security and guidance.

Curves and Corners

The easiest flat or uphill corner isn't a corner at all but merely a bend in the track. Try to ski around it by feathering the tip of the outside ski, instead of lifting skis out and clomping around. This demands some delicate heel/toe maneuvering.

On a fast downhill curve, usually a track will not have been set in the first place, or if it has, it will be quickly plowed out and a rut or bank skied into the outside of the curve. Try to ride this bank like a bobsled, driving your outside hand into the turn to help bring you around.

If you are heading downhill in a machine-set track, you can usually ride the track around gradual corners by steering with your knees. Moving the outside ski forward a bit

Use the outside snow bank to ride around. (Peter Miller)

aids steering power. To aid stability I often drag my inside pole on the snow as an outrigger. Occasionally, if the corner is faster or sharper, I'll also step out of the track with my inside ski. This gives me a wider, more secure stance while my outside ski is still stable in the track, steering me around the corner.

Crossing Fences

The next time you are confronted by a slat fence while skiing along in the countryside, don't feel intimidated — and don't bother removing your skis. There is an easier way. Just follow these simple steps by instructor Stacy Studebaker.

Ski up to the fence so that it's on your right side, with your skis parallel to the fence. Now, put both hands on the top of the fence and cross the left ski over in front of you, placing it on the lowest slat (A). Kick the right ski back and high enough to clear the top of the fence (B). Swing it over as you pivot on the left foot (C). Set the right ski down and kick the left ski back and high enough so that its tip clears the fence (D). Swing it down alongside your other ski (E).

There you have it. But I wouldn't recommend this method for clearing barbed wire!

Crossing Streams

Be careful of skiing across rivers or lakes early or late in the season, or during thaws, when the ice may be "candled" and rotten. Skis give much support, but a dousing in freezing water can be a deadly business.

You can often step across a small open stream if you establish a firm platform and steady yourself with your poles for the forthcoming hop. A more flamboyant but riskier approach calls for a double-pole plant just before the stream and a vigorous spring and vault off the poles. Timing is everything here, and knees must be loose for the landing. Rivers are another story: it's best to test them for depth with a ski pole before attempting a crossing. Go barefoot if the river is not too wide or the bed too rocky; otherwise at least remove your socks so they will be dry for further skiing on the other side. Face upstream as you

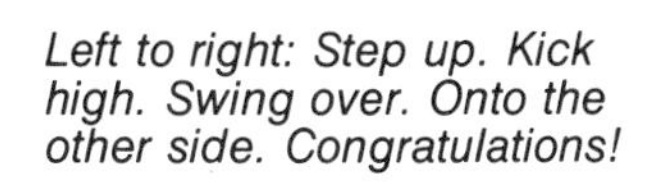

Left to right: Step up. Kick high. Swing over. Onto the other side. Congratulations!

Stream crossing: The anticipation is often worse than the doing. (Peter Miller)

work your way across, and use a ski as a steadying pole to form a secure three-point stance.

Following our 220-mile ski traverse, we descended from the high glacier plateaus of Alaska's St. Elias Range into the lowlands that spring was already embracing. Conditions deteriorated until we were forced to ski across mud flats and gravel beds, dragging our trusty supply sleds along behind, and ford rivers recently released from winter ice. We never could build up enough speed to water ski, although Steve Darrow tried it, only to have his skis quickly submerge and stick to the muddy bottom, producing a headlong dive into an icy bath! Steve emerged spouting like a wounded whale, wounded in pride only, beaching himself to dry on the sun-warmed shore.

Bushwhacking

Skiing the back country in craggy New England or the Midwest calls for some impromptu and off-beat techniques. They involve plenty of twisting, pivoting, flailing, ducking, lunging, hanging on, and corkscrewing around trees. You won't find these maneuvers discussed here or elsewhere in the literature of skiing. You don't learn *how* to flail on skinny skis, you just *do* it as snow and terrain dictate. For example, when the tight lines of unyielding spruce cramp your style, and your ski poles plunge in to the handles in the tractionless fluff, just let them dangle from

Anything goes while bushwhacking. (Ned Gillette)

wrist straps and pull yourself uphill from tree to tree like a long-toed sloth.

Pole straps come off the wrists for downhill unless you want to risk the shoulder-wrenching surprise of catching your basket on a branch. Protect your eyes by ducking and dodging among the tight branches, arms up, like a boxer. Categories of turns disappear as an upcoming maple calls for a half telemark with a skate turn followed by a jumping parallel conclusion. Call them what you will, but get around the tree.

There was no sign of a crevasse here until one of us fell in up to the armpits. (Ned Gillette)

Roped Skiing

No matter how safe and free of crevasses you *think* a glacier is, I'd recommend that you always ski roped up for safety when traveling on glaciers. Compared with foot or snowshoe travel, skis give the added advantage of distributing your weight over a larger supporting surface, thereby reducing your chance of dropping into an unseen crevasse.

I like to ski with less than half a rope length between myself and my partner, keeping the excess coiled on both our packs. Roped skiing demands close attention to pace, as the stops and starts of one skier are immediately received by the other through the umbilical safety line. This is especially critical on downhills, where a winter Laurel and Hardy act is usually the result of trying to anticipate the next turn.

Ski slowly and in control with the lead skier setting the pace. I've dropped into crevasses up to my waist but have never had the frightening and sinking feeling of dropping in deeper. As long as your skiing companion is alert and quick in reaction, it is usually possible to arrest a crevasse fall. Once in a crevasse, you can work your way up the rope to safety with a system of sliding prusik slings or mechanical ascenders.

While skiing around Mt. McKinley in 1978, we had to climb over four technically difficult passes. For safety on the way up we often set up a secure boot-axe belay in which the belayer's boot reinforces the strength and holding power of the ice axe. This is a simple belay stance which is effective, easy to learn, and fast to arrange. The descents frequently required rappelling down vertical ice cliffs. So you can see that a rope is an invaluable asset for mountain travel, for prevention of accidents, and for self-rescue.

7

COPING WITH SNOW

Tracks

Many skiers consider a pre-set ski track always the same, never changing. But think back: isn't it easier to ski the same track in some snow conditions and harder in others? Just as you might have to change your ski wax each day, so you must change your ski technique to get the most out of the day's conditions, unless you wish to be only a fair weather and packed powder skier.

Harder and faster tracks, such as hard-packed powder snow at 20°F., glazed snow, and icy snow mean faster ground speed and call for some changes in technique. When diagonal striding you can kick harder and get more carry with each stride. But often diagonal striding is not the best technique. You'll get tremendous momentum from double-poling and kick double-poling, even up some moderate hills. The tracks are unyielding grooves which

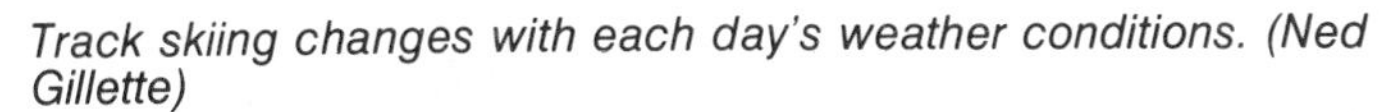

Track skiing changes with each day's weather conditions. (Ned Gillette)

(Photo at left by Ned Gillette)

secure your direction of travel. Since the baskets will not sink into the snow you can get lots of push from your poles.

Soft snow requires a very delicate technique. If you stomp down hard on the snow, it will give under your ski, causing you to slip. What you need is a change of technique which is as much a change in feeling. Don't bang uphill as you might on a firm track, but set your ski more subtly with a shorter stride. You need good balance because the sidewalls of the track are soft and will break down if your ski goes awry. Since the pole track is equally soft, preventing Herculean thrusts of the arms, you'll have to be a little less ambitious with your poling.

Slower snow requires a faster tempo to maintain your speed. Don't hang out on your gliding ski for a long time or your momentum will die. Be quick, get off that gliding ski! If the snow is super slow, use more diagonal striding on the flats. Double-poling may be useful only on gradual downhills.

Transitions

Varying snow depth: When skiing down a groomed trail, you often choose to step out into the deeper snow along the edges to slow your speed or are forced out by a trail hazard or fallen skier. This can be an explosive transition as you go abruptly from faster snow to slower snow. You must anticipate this change by sitting back just a little before you enter the powder snow.

Varying snow consistency: Sun often raises havoc with snow, changing its overall consistency in some spots on the trail more than others. Be alert to reading the track ahead so you're ready for the changes. In mid-winter the sunny areas are usually faster (powder snow with a *little* more moisture supplies more lubrication so the skis run faster). The shady areas are usually slower. However, late winter and spring conditions usually mean the opposite: the hard snow and icy areas that are shaded by trees or lie on a north-exposure slope are faster, while the sunny and south-facing slopes are slow and sticky. On downhill sections you should be ready to be pitched forward when entering a slow snow area, and set back on your heels (or elsewhere) in a fast snow area. Be crafty: look ahead and be

Be ready for transitions from fast to slow snow. (Peter Miller)

ready for the acceleration or braking action by leaning forward or sitting back.

Sitting back, by the way, preferably with the morning paper and a cup of coffee, is good strategy for the early hours of a day with good spring snow. If you venture out too early you'll be skiing, quite simply, on ice. Better to wait a couple of hours until the sun softens the snow and conditions are more inviting. At the end of the day snow can change back from mushy snow conditions into ice with a rapidity that will rattle your skis. Most types of waxless skis will not work well in these early and late hard snow conditions. So for spring skiing don't champ at the bit and don't push the day's skiing to its limits.

Icing

Just as the beauty of summer is at times compromised by the obnoxious mosquito and the tenacious black fly, so is cross-country skiing frustrated by peculiar snow conditions which often build up ice on ski bottoms. This usually occurs at that temperature most dreaded by skiers, 32°F./0°C. (freezing), when no wax seems to work and waxless skis clump up with snow.

Here are a few hints on technique which will help you ease through these trying times. To prevent the warm air from warming the ski base, thus making it more prone to icing, keep your skis pressed on the ground and sliding at all times; if you stop, move your feet in place.

Wet snow can clog skis with ice. (Ned Gillette)

Late in the winter when the sun is high, or in the Sierra of California, a new fall of powder snow gets worked over by the sun very quickly. The top inch or two of snow gets soggy, yet underneath is dry powder. Great is our woe in the face of instant icing! The trick for minimizing icing here is to keep your skis deep under the snow where it's consistently cold. Don't pick up your skis.

The sun also melts the snow on trees, dripping and causing wet areas beneath. Double-pole through these areas, then continue pressing your skis on the ground after you get back into the dryer snow to "wipe or sponge off" moisture picked up by the ski.

When skiing through the Brooks Range in 1972, we traveled mostly on frozen rivers. But the rivers were not always frozen! Often underneath secure-looking snow which covered the river ice lurked a thin layer of water. It's called overflow. If we were quick enough, sometimes we could ski through it, then right on into the super-dry snow of Arctic Alaska, "wiping" the moisture off on the dry absorbent powder without losing a stride.

Icing can be used to your advantage as well. Allowing your ski to gather a minimum amount of snow on the base gives secure grip uphill. Usually you'll be able to kick it off at the top. If not, be prepared to walk down the other side!

Tips for de-icing: Whether skiing in the East, the Rockies, or the Northwest, sooner or later we all ski through wet snow or standing water that causes ice to form on ski bottoms.

The easiest way to remove accumulated ice from ski bases without taking off skis is to scrape one ski back and forth over the other just in front of the binding. Turning the bottom ski more on edge gives it a sharper surface for removal of stubborn ice.

If you are skiing with someone, have him help by turning his own skis on edge and scraping yours over them. Scrape over a branch that is lying in the trail, or on an icy patch of snow. Sometimes severely stamping your ski down and back and forth on the trail like an angry bull will loosen ice (and possibly ease frustration). If all else fails, take off your skis and clean them with a metal or plastic scraper or with each other, or scrape them on a nearby tree.

Deep Powder

You can ski powder on cross-country skis nearly as well as you can with Alpine skis if you're experienced. Deep powder is one of life's most thrilling experiences; if you haven't tried it, you've missed the best part of skiing. My friend Terry Morse tells how he once matched downhill skiers turn for turn in knee-deep powder on thin cross-country racing skis on Prima, a steep, moguled expert trail at Vail, Colorado. He relates it with a delightful "they laughed when I sat down at the piano" grin of satisfaction.

How do you do it while skiing parallel? First, you've got to be in good physical shape because it is tiring. Second, you've got to attain some speed so your skis will float on the snow (wider skis float better). The faster you go (within reason), the more your skis will plane and the easier they will turn. Keep your weight evenly on both skis, and don't lean too far forward. Unweight severely with your knees to get around. Exaggerate your arm and pole movement to aid the unweighting. Stay in the fall line and go for it!

Telemark turns in powder are not to be passed up, and you can also do skate or step turns in deep snow, but you must be very quick in your step so you don't catch your tip in the deep stuff and go down.

Cross-country skiers have to get up the hill in all this deep snow before careening down. In deep yogurt, breaking trail can be tough. Let the ski ride up on top of the snow as you stride forward instead of physically picking it up. Be more emphatic about setting your ski on the soft snow for more grip. Neither a plodder nor a racer be: keep up a steady shuffling gait — it's less laborious than thrashing and bashing. Get your shoulders into the act for maximum pole extension.

Ice and Hard Snow

To hold on icy snow when skiing downhill is extremely difficult with cross-country skis. New skis that have acute right-angle edges not yet worn down help tremendously. You must exaggerate your edging to get all the bite and holding power possible by pushing your knees forward and into the hill for maximum edging, yet keeping your upper body leaning away from the slope so that your weight is

Cutting up powder on skinny skis. (Peter Miller)

Galen Rowell's unique method of stopping in windblown, crusty snow. (Ned Gillette)

directly over your skis throughout turns. Expect greater than the normal amount of fairly wild sliding and skidding. A sure sign that you're leaning into the turn too much with your upper body is a staccato chattering of your skis as the edges grab and let go.

Crust and Windblown Snow

These are the nastiest of all snow conditions, and my advice is simply to avoid breakable and windblown crust if at all possible. Sometimes it isn't, as at the end of our traverse of the St. Elias Range, where we encountered miles of eggshell crust. It was possibly the most frustrating skiing that I've ever encountered; we couldn't plow through it easily.

If you're faced with a downhill section, any one of a number of turns might work. One thing is for certain: you'll have to ease into them, skiing with real delicacy and poise so you'll skitter over the crust. If the crust refuses to support your weight, your only alternative is to resort to wild step turns, slow stem christies, stable telemarks, or traverses and kick turns, and accept your education as it comes.

As you can see in the photos, even Galen Rowell's "milk stool squat" was not up to handling the windblown powder of Kahiltna Pass on the flanks of Mt. McKinley, and this playful plunge ended in the surest method of stopping. Fortunately, Mr. Rowell is very durable and seems to be able to survive these flying self-arrests. I wouldn't recommend them for the average ski tourer!

Depth Hoar

Not found at the average ski touring center, this is "bottomless" snow of extraordinarily fragile crystal structure. It is created by a steep temperature gradient between extremely cold air and relatively warm ground, and it collapses under body weight. Not only does it make travel difficult, but its unstable, ball-bearing nature can make a slope susceptible to avalanches if it lies under substantial snow depth. Glacial crevasses covered by depth hoar are undistinguishable from solid surfaces, yet not supportive. My companions and I have encountered it on all major

Depth hoar: "bottomless" trail breaking. (Ned Gillette)

expeditions, and it has always forced us to leave heavy packs or sleds behind while breaking out a trail, later returning to haul our supplies. Thus each mile is covered three times. As far as I can see, depth hoar hasn't a single redeeming quality, and I introduce it to you mainly for your future avoidance.

Dudley's Crudley

Most mere mortals don't want to tackle slush, mush, Sierra cement, or mashed potato snow on 3-pin bindings. The safest way to negotiate this type of awkward snow is to traverse your way down as previously described.

Telemark turns often work, but there is a different way. I've never seen it done better than by Dudley Rood, downhill skinny-skier extraordinaire. Instead of making carved turns, Dudley simply jumps his skis up out of the snow to turn them. He calls it going weightless, and I'll let the photos speak for themselves.

Dudley's crudley. (John Dostal)

8

COPING WITH WEATHER

We have not yet discovered the Camelot of ski centers where the sun always shines, the wind never blows, and the snow is always dry and powdery. Nor have we found the one body suit functional and fashionable in all weather conditions. But recently some real progress has been made in developing clothing suitable for the wide range of conditions encountered by cross-country skiers. These new concepts have been tested in the wild climate swings of a New England winter and the penetrating dampness of the Northwest, as well as on multi-week mountaineering expeditions.

Nowhere am I more aware of the weather than on mountaineering expeditions, for there is never any retreat from it. It governs one's movements, level of comfort, margin of safety, and choice of clothing. This chapter is mainly about how to dress for skiing, but it is the *weather* that we are truly concerned with, which dictates what clothing is worn. Let's look into most of the vicissitudes of temperature, moisture, and wind that you'll be likely to meet during your skiing years.

Your aim is to maintain a comfortable body temperature throughout the day's tour. The cross-country skier is in the unique situation of having to deal with both excessive heat gain during the early energetic stages of a tour or race and excessive heat loss during the latter stages when fatigue may be high and weather conditions poor. Wearing correct clothing is as important for the tourist as it is for the racer or mountaineer. So, off with your jeans! They have a lot going for them, but not as X-C skiwear.

Rule number one: Don't overdress. Until you've seen for yourself just how warm you can get cross-country skiing, take my advice and stay clear of heavy, bulky clothing. It is not uncommon for a Trapp instructor, wearing what appears to be little more than a jogging suit on a cold morn-

There are lots of choices in cross-country clothing – you don't have to be fancy to be comfortable. (Peter Miller)

ing, to meet a class which appears to be dressed for an assault on the West Ridge of Everest. This down-filled quilted excess simply will not do. Not only is it hard to ski looking like the Michelin Man, but it's a guarantee of an immediate overheating of your engine and a sloshing sweat bath.

The secret is layering so you can tailor your dress to the needs of the moment according to the demands of exertion and weather. Rather than one heavy layer of clothing, you should aim for several layers of lighter items. These different layers trap the warm air your body produces. (Clothing fibers do not insulate; it's the trapped air in and between layers.) Layering enables you to remove a veneer or two to allow heat and moisture to escape. When you rest for an extended period and start to cool down, simply compensate by putting on extra layers. Consider how uncomfortably you would sleep if you utilized only one great down quilt all year round.

Your clothing should fit your body without pressing or binding in any one place, making it uncomfortable or reducing the blood supply to your extremities. It should be designed to allow freedom of movement. It should be of breathable material so your body moisture can escape but tightly woven so water and snow will roll off and wind will be cut. "Light is right," since insulation is proportional to thickness, not weight. Check that your clothing covers the critical freezing points: head, neck, wrists, waist, ankles. Select ski wear that has flexibility so that different combinations will allow you to dress for touring, racing, multiday tours, and off-season jogging and bicycling.

The watchword is function with style. Good manufacturers first build a suit that has functionality, then add the style. There is a difference between those *planning* to be in bad weather and those *surprised* by bad weather. Surprised ones are in trouble in poorly designed clothing.

It is not only in bad weather that experienced skiers will carry some extra clothing along or take time to make small adjustments in what they are wearing. John Dostal learned to ski in the Sierra and still packs Sierra-conditioned extras on a long New England tour. For instance, skiing up Vermont's Mt. Mansfield for a spring run down closed trails was sweaty business, so running suit top

Layers allow you to tailor your clothing. (Michael Brady)

was stashed and hat came off. As is usually the case, the higher up you go the colder it gets and the more the wind kicks up. A wind shell was welcome, as were dry gloves and liners to replace those sweat-drenched from uphill work. Dressing in anticipation for the kind of tour you'll be on is what matters. At the base of Mt. Mansfield it would have been shorts and T-shirts all day.

Your personal guideline should be to avoid both sweating and feeling chilled. Adjust your clothing immediately at the first sign of either. Sweating can reduce the insulative value of your clothing to 10 percent of its original value. Change your clothing as soon as possible after skiing, or at least put on a dry shirt. Chilling can increase your oxygen consumption by 50 percent, and shivering can lead to exhaustion. Exposure to wind sucks heat from the body unbelievably quickly.

For long multi-week expeditions I have been going increasingly toward the use of synthetics, which are light, strong, and warm, and dry quickly. On my first expedition in 1972 I wore mostly wool, down, and a little cotton. Now I wear hardly any natural fiber except occasionally a down parka, wool mitts, and wool socks. (Even the socks are partially nylon.) Maybe the trend will reverse, but now I'm very satisfied with the performance of synthetics: fiberpile jackets and mitts, Polarguard or Thinsulite parkas, nylon wind shells, polypropylene underwear, Gore-Tex anorak and wind pants. The most exciting new garment I've tested is a specially designed full-length bib-top expedition and touring suit, of acrylic nylon on the outside backed by a thin veneer of wool on the inside. Of four-way stretch material, it is very light yet warm, highly water-resistant, and 97 percent windproof, yet it still breathes. It is close to the ideal fabric for tour skiers as well as expedition members. You can see what possibilities synthetics bring to the ski-wear scene.

The Layers

1. **Transportation:** Starting from the inside out, your first layer should keep you dry, allowing sweat to escape and evaporate so you don't feel soaked during or after skiing. There is only one thing that really works: super underwear made of polypropylene. It's plastic underwear but with the look and feel of woven cotton — the one piece of clothing on which I insist. We used it for 90 days straight on the Ellesmere Island Expedition. Ski racers at all levels favor it, and it's being discovered by road runners and cyclists as well. It is an alternative to nothing because it works like nothing else. Because it's nonabsorbent, moisture is pushed through to the next layer so there is always a dry layer next to your skin. Trapp instructors doing

Practical clothing for moving freely. (Ned Gillette)

yearly penance at the 60 km Vermont Ski Marathon come in with sweat-soaked hats, shirts, and ski suits and their polypropylene underwear still dry.

2. **Insulation:** Nothing much new here. A turtleneck shirt is still the old standby because it breathes, soaks up sweat, and keeps the neck protected. For spring skiing, try a T-shirt instead.

3. **Action:** This is the layer which will be on the outside for most of your skiing. It should stretch or be loose enough for free movement and be warm for its light weight. Water resistance is desirable, combined with breathability as well as some wind protection. This could be a one- or two-piece suit of acrylic nylon, cotton-nylon combination, high-quality poplin, or thin wool (wool insulates even when wet). Knickers and knee-length socks or full-length jogging suits are your best bets for your lower body. Socks should be a flat, tight weave of wool or wool and nylon (bulky socks pick up and retain too much snow). Bib knickers are a good compromise between one-piece suits and waist knickers: they are comfortable and eliminate the gap between jacket and knickers. Don't be afraid of investing

Wind protection. (Galen Rowell)

in a one-piece ski suit; I guarantee you'll feel better and ski better. Many one-piece suits are available in non-flash Clark Kent colors.

4. **Protection:** This is your layer of last resort. It keeps the wind and rain out of your insulating layers. Carry this extra insurance tied around your waist or in your rucksack. You have many choices here, the best of which is an anorak, wind parka, or lined warm-up suit that is big enough to fit outside and over your other layers. Second choices are parkas, vests, and sweaters.

Extreme Cold

During the 1979 bone-freezing pre-Olympic meet in Lake Placid, temperatures dropped to 10 below zero F.

Most competitors added extra clothing to protect themselves during their all-out efforts. A few toughened racers seemed not to notice the cold, led by a giant bearded Finn named Juha Mieto, who raced the 15-kilometer cross-country course with bare hands. Mieto was later one-upped by Russian Nikolai Zimyatov, who not only skied the course without gloves but was said to have done it without underwear as well. Neither option do I recommend for the average touring skier of sound mind.

It was not uncommon during these races to see competitors finish with white hardened patches on cheeks, nose, and earlobes. This is frostnip and should not be ignored. It can be thawed out with the warmth of a hand without tissue damage. A super-cold day at touring centers is an occasion for some frosty socializing as passing skiers alert each other to evident frostnip. Don't shy away from skiing on a crackling cold day. A little extra care in dressing will ensure a pleasant tour.

Starting from the bottom, don't cram extra socks into your shoes for cold weather, as they'll cut off blood circulation. Leave plenty of room to wiggle your toes. Try one of the commercially available lined overboots, designed to let the boot still fit into the binding. Or pull an old wool sock over your ski boot and jam the whole rig into your binding. The sock will ball up with snow but your feet will remain warm.

Overboots for super-warm feet. (Ned Gillette)

Cold feet are a common complaint with many cross-country skiers. Most have probably dressed for skiing long before they've gotten out on the trail so that their socks are already soaked with perspiration. For warmer feet, start out with dry, clean socks.

Wear gaiters (like 1920s spats) for deep-snow plunging. Snow clings to knee socks, then has the unpleasant habit of melting and running into your shoes. Gaiters help prevent soggy socks.

On a cold day fast skiers may be able to get by with gloves as long as they've added a wool liner. But mittens are much warmer. Use wool mitts with a separate outer shell or nylon mitts with a synthetic pile lining. Down mitts are OK if you're training for the Golden Gloves but too bulky for X-C skiing.

Still, your hands may get cold now and then. Windmill your arms vigorously in big circles to push the blood into your fingertips. Stay with it for several minutes until your fingers warm up and tingle or until you are airborne.

Speaking of cold hands, it is strangely necessary to turn to noses at the same time. It is not uncommon at Trapp's to see touring skiers take off mittens or gloves in subzero cold to extract a tissue from the inner reaches of their garments. As Dostal observes, once used, the tissue has become a sodden wad in the pocket or, discarded, a ski-slowing mound in the track. Much better to resort to the St. Nick trick. Lay a finger alongisde *your* nose, lean over to clear your skis, and blow through the unweighted nostril. Be assured that in the etiquette of cross-country skiing such a means of discharge is entirely proper.

Your head is the body's most efficient radiator, able to radiate up to 75 percent of the total amount of body heat loss. So, the old saying, "When your feet are cold, put on a hat," is really valid. If you're skiing vigorously, a lightweight hat is your best choice. If it's super-cold, two hats are entirely legitimate. Or use a tight-fitting headband or earband under your regular hat to prevent frostnip of the earlobes. A balaclava (wool helmet) which covers your entire head except your eyes, nose, and mouth supplies great protection, as does a handkerchief tied over the face. Both are good rigs for beginning a life of crime.

Last but not least, a word to the gents. How shall I say

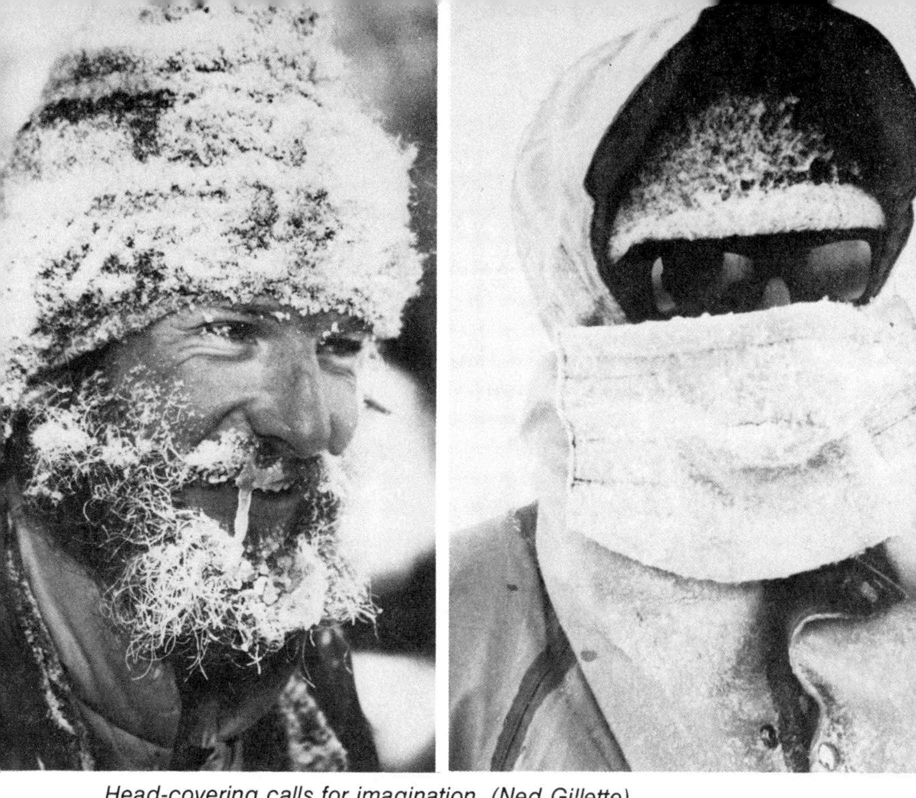

Head-covering calls for imagination. (Ned Gillette)

this? **Protect your parts!** Groinal frostnip has unfortunately been well documented in medical literature. One company named Lifa makes special jockey shorts with a windproof panel of nylon in front. I call them "fig Lifas." Lacking them, almost anything will do for a Nordic codpiece: a sock, a hat, the *New York Times,* birch bark. . . . Ladies, ski on! To my knowledge you have no corresponding difficulties.

Wind

The tricks of dressing for extreme cold will protect you from wind as well. For your face you may want to add a hood that is big enough to protect you from a side wind, or a face mask or goggles, so that not even your closest friend will recognize you!

Your chief shield against wind is a good-quality anorak or wind parka. But many garments which profess to be windproof just plain are not. Check them out by blowing through them onto your hand. Is there much resistance? Remember that air is a good insulator as long as it is not moving. So wind-protective garments should keep trapped air next to your body.

Rain and Wet Snow

Avoid getting wet at all costs. It is much more dangerous for you to be wet out on the trail than to be cold in a dry climate: it's easier to warm yourself up than to dry out, a fact verified by all who ski in the Northwest. Even though

Sunny weather is a mixed blessing on expeditions. (Ned Gillette)

the temperature may be above freezing, you can become chilled and helpless in a remarkably short period of time.

A raincoat or cagoule that is totally waterproof is fine to ski in it if is big enough to ventilate from the bottom. Be careful not to ski so fast that you get a drenching in your own sweat. Better is an outer shell made of Gore-Tex or a similar breathable but waterproof material. Or wear a couple of layers that you feel you can afford to get wet, then change immediately to clothing you have kept dry in a plastic bag in your rucksack. Keep a pair of mittens and socks dry as well.

Heat

Since we usually think of needing protection from cold and driving wind, it sounds strange that we must be careful of serious overexposure to the sun while skiing. In the spring, when the sun is blistering, excess heat can be a major problem, especially at high altitudes, when you can sunburn the roof of your mouth while glacier skiing! It is easy to be deceived about the amount of sun you are getting in the chilled high mountain air. Discard layers of clothing, but consider keeping one light layer on as a sun shield, as the Arabs do. Wear dark glasses, a hat with a sun visor, and plenty of sun screen applied imaginatively — remember that the sun is reflecting off the snow and can burn earlobes and armpits. Drink plenty of water to prevent dehydration. Sun stroke will incapacitate you just as much as extreme shivering.

(Ned Gillette)

9

WINTER SURVIVAL

You and two friends are 6 miles from the road, night is falling, it is snowing. You have been touring all day with some clothing and accessories in your small day pack. And now you have the unsettling suspicion that you're about to become part of a Jack London story.

Apprehension is difficult to deal with as darkness approaches. Keep your head about you and think your next moves through carefully. Stay together and don't be hesitant about spending the night out if reasonable alternatives of escape are slim. Even with a headlamp your chances of getting out safely in the dark are much less than of getting lost and expending valuable energy foolishly. To plunge forward wishfully may only increase your error. You can be quite comfortable if you follow a few simple guidelines. (And you might have avoided the entire situation if you had judged your speed of travel more realistically and turned back while there was still ample light.)

Carefully inventory your personal possessions and analyze how each might help you. Socks don't always go on the feet in a situation like this — they're good mitts as well. Consider using shoestring or belts for rope, skis and poles for building shelter, backpack to stuff your feet into, shoes to sit on, ski tip as a shovel, ski tail to cut snow blocks, ace bandages from a first-aid kit to keep head, feet, or hands warm, and tape as string. Put on any extra clothing as soon as you stop, especially dry socks and a dry layer next to your skin and an outer layer for wind and water protection. Conserve as much heat as possible right from the beginning.

Start looking for a spot to bivouac as soon as possible. Scout out the surrounding area thoroughly in 10 to 15 minutes for the best shelter site: a big boulder for wind protection, a log to crawl under. The conical depression in the snow around a tree with branches fanning out above is good shelter, as is a snow bank to dig into. Snow is a wonderful insulator, and a shallow trench dug with skis

Be innovative in finding a shelter. (Wayne Merry)

and hands and covered with tarp held down by skis makes a comfortable little niche in a stormy situation, as long as you've avoided windy ridges and gullies where cold air settles.

Locate dry tinder, dead wood, or bark for fire starter. The inner lower dead branches of evergreen trees are usually dry even in the worst weather. A big factor in the success of fire starting is an extended search for good wood; take the time while you can still see. A short candle stub will help start the flames. Locate the fire so that snow from overlying branches won't kill it. Build it on a rock if possible to prevent it from melting into the snow, and use a rock, a log, or banked snow as a reflector. You have a choice of building a small, efficient fire to keep warm by or a big bonfire that'll keep you warm running for firewood.

I recall a couple who were benighted on the trail coming in to return two pairs of nicely roasted and charred rental skis, along with melted boots, to the Yosemite Mountaineering School. Although they built a fire from available forest wood, they confessed to adding their skis from time to time. Normally it's not such a hot idea to burn your means of transportation. Fortunately they left enough of the skis intact so they could ski out the next morning. (Incidentally, you need matches to start fires. If you've forgotten them or they're not waterproof, you'll have plenty of time during the cold night ahead to contemplate your oversight.)

Create a bed or sitting platform from dead branches, meadow grass, backpack, rope, or small foam pad (if you've gone touring prepared) to cut loss of heat via conduction.

Eat whatever food you wish that evening if you feel assured you'll get out the next day; you'll need the heating calories to stay warm during the night. Drink plenty of water if available, as it's easy to become dehydrated. Eating snow will take the dry sticky taste out of your mouth but contribute little toward rehydrating. Icicles can sometimes be found.

So just settle in like a Neanderthal and make the best of the situation. Remember two bodies huddling together are better than one! Rest assured that plenty of other people have made it through unprotected nights in the winter.

As a postscript, if your companion is injured and unable to travel, the best tack is to make him or her warm, dry, and comfortable (after administering the necessary first aid), and go for help if adequate daylight remains. In the event that you do have to haul an injured skier to safety, it is possible to construct an emergency toboggan out of one or more sets of skis.

Yosemite Lesson

Jeff and I decided to ski the 25 miles from Yosemite Valley to Tuolumne Meadows in one day, a gain of 5,000 feet (to 9,000 feet) with lots of undulation in between. We carried moderately heavy packs, planning to stay for a week and do some winter climbing. Starting at daybreak we sped up the steep 3,000-foot climb out of the Valley, full

Still-smiling novices at Tenaya Lake, Yosemite. (Don Mossman)

of enthusiasm and energy. Donna joined us at the Snowcreek cabin, located at the top of the valley wall. We continued on in fine shape, the goal of making Tuolumne in one day fixed rigidly in our minds. The trail-breaking was difficult but not impossible in typically heavy Sierra snow.

Several miles farther on, at Tenaya Lake, we discovered that we possessed only one quart of water for all of us! (This was our first clue that we should have altered our plans, but it was overlooked in our novice enthusiasm.) We continued on with the sweaty work, now without water, becoming acutely dehydrated. As the sun hit the horizon, we were only about four miles short of our destination. A brief discussion was held about stopping and bivouacking, but with no tent and with the lure of a warm and snug cabin beckoning us onward, we set off again along the unplowed road, just able to find our way as darkness settled over us at 5:30 p.m.

I can remember feeling a bit dizzy and fuzzy-headed as we pressed on, now committed to our personal marathon. The snow continued to be difficult to plow through, and our pace slowed. We had overestimated our remaining strength. The final few miles seemed to take forever. At 9 p.m. — 16 hours after starting — we arrived in Tuolumne, staggering along like mechanical toys at a snail's pace, lurching onto our poles for balance. We were dog-tired, in the initial stages of hypothermia, and desperately in need of water. Stopping at a bridge where the road crossed the river, we could hear water gurgling. I took off my skis, grabbed my ice axe, and crawled under the bridge onto the clean ice. Like a madman I beat and hammered the ice in an attempt to break through to the water. Sparks flew, but I was too far gone to heed their message, and it was not until later that I realized that I had been hitting rocks.

Then, as if I'd been shocked by a bolt of lightning, I was alert and in command again. Jeff had just announced that he couldn't feel his toes, and hadn't for a couple of hours. I was up on the road, into my skis, and charging across the meadow toward the Park Service cabin. It was locked. Where would they hide a key? Unusually clever, we located it within five minutes, burst in, started the stove, heated water to drink and, alas, to thaw out Jeff's toes, which were waxy white and hard as wood.

Lukewarm water at 108°F., accompanied by bite-the-bullet pain, brought the feet back to life, but it was obvious that Jeff was a stretcher case and would not ski out, since feet, once thawed, will suffer tissue damage if walked on. (If self-evacuation is absolutely necessary for a limited distance, do it on still-frozen feet for safety.) The cabin telephone still worked, and a rescue was carried out by the Park Service the following day.

Through inexperience, we never foresaw the repercussions of our risky enterprise and didn't take precautionary steps until the situation was critical (although after realizing at the end that we really were in trouble we did take cool and resolute steps). As Lito Tejada-Flores states, "The role of judgment and preparedness is to *reduce* the likelihood or magnitude of such an accident, not to eliminate the risk altogether. It simply cannot be done." (*Wilderness Skiing,* published by the Sierra Club.)

Risks shouldn't be taken in wilderness travel unless absolutely necessary. We extended our physical resources to the limit, bringing on extraordinary fatigue, when there was no emergency and a secure bivouac short of our goal was possible. We made ourselves vulnerable to committing mistakes of judgment and coordination. This we initiated by starting out too quickly first thing in the morning, which caused us to perspire freely, losing valuable water and saturating our clothes.

We all assumed that others had the essential equipment (like water and extra socks) without ever double-checking.

Even though a stove and pot were handy in our packs, we never took the time to stop and brew up. Acute dehydration closed in and appetite was lost as thirst grew, contributing to low blood sugar and slackened energy, which in turn led toward the initial stages of hypothermia.

Jeff wore inflexible mountain boots with cable bindings. Although not always the case, on this occasion lack of the flexing action of an ordinary cross-country shoe caused his feet to freeze, while Donna's and mine were OK. The lack of food and water was another major factor in his susceptibility to frostbite. He didn't tell us soon enough that he was having foot problems, and we assumed his feet were in the same condition as ours. Nobody stopped to change to dry socks during the day. (We did thaw his feet out properly, and although the healing was lengthy, Jeff lost no toes.)

We grossly miscalculated our possible rate of travel as night approached. We were fatigued in body and mind and our last miles were increasingly slow and tortuous.

Our goal of getting to the cabin in one day and finishing what we set out to do clouded our reasoning. We paid the price of inflexible thinking and inconvenienced scores of people in the Park Service.

You don't have to be doing big trips in big mountains to take the proper precautions or get into trouble. Daily trail sweeps at Trapp's often disclose ill-prepared skiers who are lost or overly fatigued even on well-marked trails. The result is usually acute discomfort. But further out on our unpatrolled wilderness trails the stakes are even higher on a cold January night or rainy March afternoon.

More on Hypothermia

Our ill-fated ski trip in Yosemite led us into the initial stages of hypothermia. In its acute stage it is an extremely common cause of death in the outdoors. The skier shivering at the end of the day in soaked blue jeans and thin wet gloves is headed for hypothermia. If that skier is within easy distance of a touring center or farmhouse, it is not as dangerous as if he had to pass the night in a tent. A friend once skied across the Sierra with two out-of-shape skiers who overextended the first day and were so hypothermic that they couldn't understand simple directions on how to help put up a tent. The wind wasn't blowing, they weren't wet, but they had simply burned all their fuel and gotten cold quickly.

Prolonged exposure to cold (not necessarily below 32°F./0°C.), wind and wet, and lack of preparation can cause a lowering of the temperature of the body's core. Heat loss by the body exceeds heat production. If the temperature falls below a certain point, the process is irreversible and death follows. Symptoms vary with different

You can be very comfortable in snow if you play it smart. (Galen Rowell)

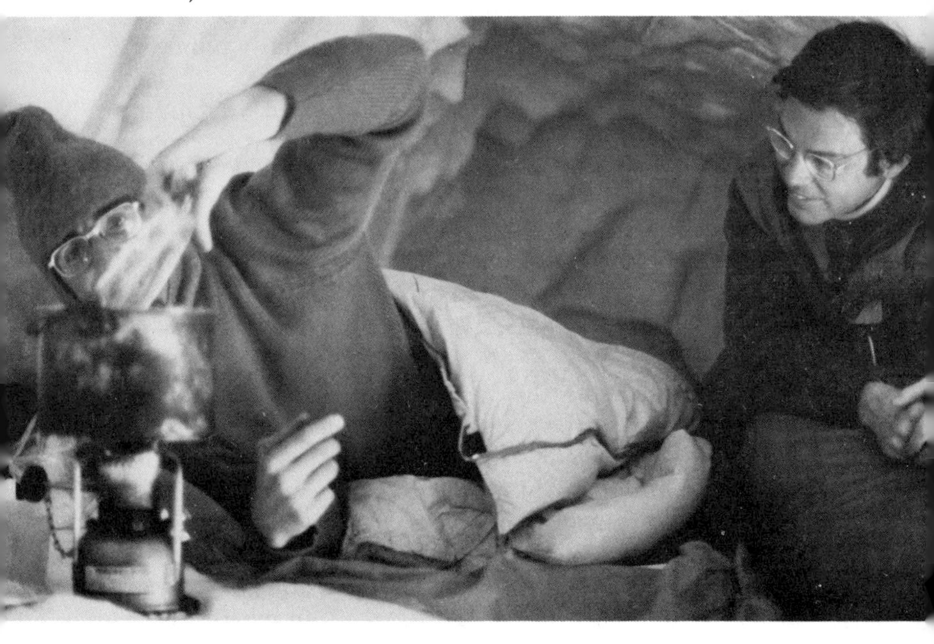

persons, but the most common are intense shivering, fatigue, numbness, poor coordination, stumbling pace, impaired speech, weak pulse, blue lips, tense muscles, and irrational thought. Treat by preventing further loss of body heat, then adding warmth. This means you must find shelter, replace wet clothing with dry and add layers of insulation, get the victim into a pre-warmed sleeping bag, build a fire, surround him with warm bodies, give him hot drinks and get him into a hot bath if possible. Avoid alcohol, which leads to additional heat loss by dilating blood vessels, and tobacco, which reduces circulation in the extremities. Core temperatures below 90°F. are critical, and quick action must be taken to save lives.

The best way to defend against hypothermia is to avoid the problem by dressing properly and not overextending, rather than treating it once it occurs. Be careful not to underestimate the extent to which wetness and wind accelerate heat loss.

Acute Mountain Sickness

This is common above 7,000 feet. Headache, nausea, perhaps vomiting, and shortness of breath usually improve after a day or two. Fluids, aspirin, and limited activity are the best treatments. Descent is usually unnecessary.

High-altitude pulmonary edema is caused by gaining elevation too quickly, and is far more serious than mountain sickness. It can happen at elevations of 10,000 feet and above. Dr. Charles Houston, noted expert on the body's reaction to altitude, writes, "Altitude illness kills the young, the fit, and the audacious, because they are the people who go into the mountains. Pulmonary edema occurs when blood serum seeps from the lung's capillaries into the tiny air sacs, or alveoli, which they surround. As fluid accumulates in the air sacs, the transfer of oxygen and carbon dioxide between lungs and blood is disrupted. Lack of oxygen develops rapidly, further aggravating the problem. The victim literally drowns in his own juices unless drastic measures are taken. Weakness, shortness of breath, increasing cough begin 12 to 48 hours after too rapid ascent and progress to coma and death. No medication, no treatment — not even oxygen — can substitute for getting down to the richer oxygen supply at lower altitudes. Waiting to see what weather or medication will bring can be fatal. The best and only way to prevent high-altitude illness is to take time to climb." (From "High," in *Backpacker* magazine #27.)

Navigation

The serious wilderness skier should take a topographic map on all long tours. Learn to visualize the terrain by quick interpretation of the contour lines so you can choose the path of least resistance for travel. Orient the map to line it up with visual landmarks before using it, or use a compass to align the map. I've found that I use a compass very infrequently, even on long expeditions. If the weather is bad enough to have to use a compass, I seldom travel. Try to keep in your mind a clear idea of the terrain you have recently passed in case of a forced retreat, and a general

Use a compass if visual landmarks are poor. (Ned Gillette)

Tell-tale signs of a skier's passing. (John Fuller)

idea of the distance covered. Roads, rivers, powerlines, etc., that run parallel to your route are easily located by sharply angling your direction.

If you come across ski tracks and wonder which direction the skier has taken, look at the tracks that the pole has left in the snow. Planting the pole usually leaves a tail on the back of the basket imprint as the skier moves forward.

The position of the sun gives a good idea of direction. You can find south by pointing the hour hand of your watch toward the sun; halfway between the hour hand and 12 is south. (Digital watches won't give a very satisfying readout here!) Navigate by the North Star, and remember that in Orion, the uppermost of the three stars in the belt rises due east and sets due west from any point on Earth.

Whiteouts

While skiing across the polar ice shelf that protrudes from the north shore of Ellesmere Island at 83° north latitude, we encountered extreme whiteout conditions caused by the leads opening up in the Arctic Ocean.

Whiteout: where snow and sky are the same.
(Ned Gillette)

Visibility was severely reduced. Our normal sense of direction, movement, and balance was lost. There were no landmarks — everything was white, and our compass was not dependable that close to the North Pole. A system of navigation was finally worked out using the occasional glimpses of the oily sun to orient ourselves generally for a certain hour of the day. As the sun moved we adjusted the angle at which we kept it for guidance. To keep ourselves on a straight line of travel when the sun was hidden, the four of us separated as much as possible while still maintaining visual and voice contact. The last man in line could sight ahead and determine departures to the left or right.

Fog, blizzards, and heavy rain make traveling difficult whatever the surrounding terrain. Featureless terrain adds to your disorientation. The combination of whiteout and lack of landmarks can lead to unpleasant consequences. Not only is it easy to lose your sense of direction and perspective of size, but you just plain cannot distinguish dips, bumps, steepness of slopes or their runout, lips of cliffs, crevasses, or glaciers. I recall coming within a couple of feet of skiing into a crevasse big enough to gobble up several boxcars near Mt. McKinley. Avoid that sinking feeling in whiteout conditions — be overly cautious.

Avalanches

Let's hope none of us ever gets caught in an avalanche. I will relay a few points from the U.S. Forest Service on avoiding and surviving snow avalanches. For more detailed information, you should refer to Ed LaChapelle's *The ABC of Avalanche Safety,* published by The Mountaineers.

Loose-snow avalanches start at a point and grow in size. Slab avalanches start when a large area of snow begins to slide at once. Practically all accidents are caused by slabs, many times triggered by the victims themselves. Convex slopes of 30° to 45° steepness are most prone to slides. North-facing slopes are most likely to go in midwinter, while south-facing slopes are dangerous because wind-deposited snow adds depth and creates hard, hollow-sounding wind slabs. Large rocks, trees, and heavy brush help anchor snow, but avalanches can start virtually anywhere.

Avalanches are exciting from a distance, but this one was too close for comfort. (Ned Gillette)

Weather factors: The nature of the underlying old snow surface is important: rough compacted surfaces favor stability, smooth crusty surfaces are unstable. Sustained winds of 15 mph or more cause dangerous rapid buildups on leeward slopes. Eighty percent of all avalanches occur during or just after storms, and snow falling at 1 inch per hour or more is to be watched carefully. Small crystals (needles and pellets) are more likely to slide than the usual star-shaped crystals (check out crystal shapes by letting them fall on a dark ski mitt). Snow persists in an unstable condition in cold temperatures. It will settle and stabilize rapidly near freezing. Storms starting with low temperatures and dry snow followed by rising temperatures are most likely to cause avalanches. The dry snow at the start forms a poor bond and has insufficient strength to support the heavier snow deposited later in the storm.

Beware when snowballs or "cartwheels" roll down the slope or when the snow sounds hollow and snow cracks run. Avoid old avalanche paths. Travel on the windward side of ridge tops away from cornices, or far out in the valley. If you must cross dangerous slopes, stay high. Avoid zigzagging across dangerous slopes on ascents and descents. Take advantage of areas of dense timber, ridges, or rocky outcrops as islands of safety. Only one person at a time should cross a dangerous slope; all others should watch him. Remove ski pole straps and ski safety straps, loosen all equipment, put on mitts and cap, and fasten clothing. Carry and use an avalanche cord or, much better, an avalanche radio beacon — a tiny radio transmitter which can be turned over to "receive," thus enabling survivors to locate a buried victim.

Fortunately, I have no personal experience to draw on, but if you're unlucky enough to be caught in an avalanche, discard all equipment, try to stay on top by "swimming," and work your way to the side if possible. Before coming to a stop, get your hands in front of your face and try to make an air space. Remain calm!

If you're a survivor, check for further slide danger, then mark the place where you last saw the victim. Search for him or pieces of equipment directly downslope from the last seen point. If he is not on the surface, scuff or probe the snow with a ski pole or stick. You are the victim's best hope for survival, so don't desert him and go for help unless help is only a few minutes away. The buried victim has only a 50 percent chance of surviving after one hour.

The general rule of thumb in the mountains is to never totally extend and commit yourself unless it is absolutely necessary or the goal justifies the risk (which it seldom does). However, once in a great while you choose to go for it, and with luck and careful calculation based on experience, extreme accomplishments far beyond normal limits have a chance of success.

In June, 1978, Galen Rowell had the idea that Mt. McKinley could be climbed in a day from 10,000-foot Kahiltna Pass if everything went right — us, the snowpack on the trail, and the weather. McKinley had never

Galen Rowell on the summit ridge of Mt. McKinley. (Ned Gillette)

before been approached in this way. It was a long shot, but he had it exactly calculated. I agreed to go along. After a climb more exhausting than we thought possible, we stood on the 20,320-foot summit on one of those rare still days of brilliant sunshine at the top of North America. Without the gift of perfect weather, either the climb would have been aborted at the lower elevations or I would not be writing this book today.

10

WILDERNESS TOURING

Ahead lay the Robeson Channel, a narrow splinter of the ocean separating Ellesmere Island and Greenland at 82° north latitude. It seemed as if the devil himself had been at work here. Ocean currents and wind had created a confusion of ice so forbidding that often it appeared totally impossible that a sled route could be found. Pressure ridges up to 30 feet in height were connected with a chaotic maze of smaller ice chunks. On shore, 1,500-foot black cliffs rose directly above the pack ice. Infrequent level corridors along the shore provided the only alternative to forced travel on the ocean ice.

Seventy-five years ago Robert Peary had been turned back by the ice of the Robeson Channel. It hadn't been attempted for more than fifty years. Now it lay before us, ominous and silent. The channel was the greatest uncertainty of our circular route; failure here would necessitate aborting the entire expedition.

It was even more difficult than we'd anticipated. The flat pans of ice made good sledging, but they were few and far between. We tried to avoid the chaos of the ice jumbles; they slowed our progress to a mere crawl. When detour was impossible, we had no choice but to launch a forward attack on the pressure ridges. We'd climb to the top of the highest pressure ridge to look ahead, but often no obvious route could be detected. In that case, our sleds were left behind and scouts sent ahead to find a passage through the icy maze. With patience we could piece the puzzle together and lay out a route. Then each man harnessed himself to his 240-pound sled and waged an individual battle on the unyielding ice.

The sleds seemed to have minds of their own. After we had strained with every ounce of our strength to pull them up to the top of an ice ridge, their weight, suddenly released to descend the other side, would jam us helplessly

Travel was spectacular but easy on Ellesmere Island. . .

forward, pinning us against the next obstacle. We marveled that the sleds didn't disintegrate completely as they crashed down onto the rock-hard ice. Time after time two, three, and even all four of us had to manhandle the heavy sleds one by one over particularly severe jumbles of ice. Polar bear tracks were occasionally sighted in the new snow between the pinnacles of ice.

Every evening we stopped dog-tired. Every morning as we harnessed ourselves to the sleds it seemed impossible that we'd be able to pull through another day. But the channel, more than any other part of the expedition, hammered us together into a working team. This was the most difficult traveling of the whole route, and the challenge knit us into a truly effective unit that could cope with anything, expected or not.

Multi-week ski expeditions are an aspect of cross-country skiing which appeals to many in their dreams but few in practice. Except for the level of commitment and the

. . .Easy, that is, until we were forced into the ice pack. (Ned Gillette)

amount of organizing involved, they are really little different from the weekend overnights many of us go on at least a few times during our skiing lives. Truthfully, the hardest part of an expedition is deciding that it is the thing you most want to do. Everything else follows relatively easily.

You don't have to travel thousands of miles to get a true wilderness experience. With a little imagination and research, it is possible to head off the beaten track and on your own in every part of Canada and the United States. Though I was brought up in Vermont, my first twenty years of skiing were limited to Alpine lift yo-yoing (which I still thoroughly enjoy) and cross-country racing. I never considered using skis as tools of transportation. Following several years in the West and several long ski expeditions, I returned to Vermont and discovered a whole new world of off-track skiing in my own backyard.

For longer trips, many places in the West, Canada, and Alaska are brimming with possibilities for long ski trips. Most can be done with friends for relatively little money. If you feel unsure of yourself, start with long one-day tours with experienced companions. The long treks have their own magic, and they're worth all the hours and hours of organization. For me, being out in wild areas for an extended period allows my cares and patterns of normal existence to fade away, leaving me free to enjoy the rhythm of the land. This is what expeditions are really all about — the joy and simplicity of being outdoors.

Off-track day tours, overnights, Alpine touring, ski mountaineering, expeditions: all offer the common challenge of coping with more variability of terrain, snow conditions and weather than one encounters in lift-assisted or touring center skiing (though these practice slopes and commercial ski trails can be stepping stones of confidence from which to move into the mountains). Steep icy headwalls of ancient cirques test the skier's mettle, as do breakable crust and deep powder. Pulling across a vast, snow-covered plain into the biting teeth of a brisk northerly with no sheltering rock or tree in sight demands the resolution of the marathon runner. The onslaught of darkness with three hours of traveling still ahead demands an experienced mind to control a wild imagination and a fatigued body. These journeys into a frozen land, deep in hibernation, are at times frustrating, tedious, grueling, cold, and seemingly too much trouble. You are unrealistic if you think you'll always avoid cold, unworkable hands and the trauma of breaking trail in heavy, soggy, cement-like snow. It is all to be expected. Accepted. And it can be horribly exasperating in its fickleness. But then the sun comes out, or that long-sought-after bowl of sheltered powder is cut with your telemark alone, or the stove finally heats the tea water, or you're laughing over that same ridiculous joke with your mates. It is curious how we remember only the good times of our past treks, and our selective memories always draw us back for more of the reality of being out on our own — committed, self-sufficient, curiously and simply challenged.

Guidelines for the Outback

Over the years I've developed a few guidelines which help ensure the success of my expeditions. They're appli-

Mount St. Elias, Alaska. (Ned Gillette)

cable to your tours as well, regardless of their length in days or miles.

1. Plan the trip to be fun: an adventurous vacation if you will, among friends. There is some very hard work involved, the usual physical discomfort, and mental strain; but overall we always have a great time!

2. Small, competent parties multiply strength and security and allow fast travel. More than four members on ski trips merely adds more chances for errors and injuries. Speed is your primary margin of safety. There are dangerous areas along most extended routes, across which you must go as quickly as possible. While circling Mt. McKinley we had no alternative but to rappel from Traleika Divide, a steep 1,500-foot slope with a southern exposure, underlain by ice. The sun roasted the route, and we were giddy with apprehension that the entire slope might slide. "Get on with it early in the morning and get off it quickly" was our guideline.

Grown men celebrate the author's birthday at 83° north latitude – expedition banquet style. (Ned Gillette)

3. Determine everyone's expectations. Does one want to photograph primarily while the other two want to press forward and make miles? Different goals create friction, hamstringing the competence of a party. On my first expedition across the Brooks Range, Wayne and Jed wanted to relax and do some climbing for fun in the mountains along the way. I was super goal-oriented and wanted to press forward at all costs, completing our original plan to ski all the way to the Arctic Ocean across the North Slope. Jack was happy to be in the mountains and do either. Great arguments ensued, mostly due to my inexperienced bullheadedness. It was needless. Plan a strategy before the trip and pick people who are going the same direction.

4. Know the people you are traveling with, both their strong and their weak points. Off-track skiing is no place to get caught with incompetent traveling mates or those that crack mentally under pressure. You may have to depend on each other for your lives, as Galen Rowell and I did during our abortive first attempt to climb Mt. McKinley in one day. Our rocketing fall, roped together, was arrested by a desperate grasp for an old fixed rope left by previous climbers. Six more feet and we would have slid over the ice cliff. Galen's face was badly cut and bleeding profusely; he

Moving on. (Peter Miller)

went immediately into shock. We were totally tangled and precariously balanced on the tip of disaster, so that one false move by either of us would have ended it all. Galen functioned magnificently, and the retreat, although painful, was without further major incident (except my tumble into a crevasse).

5. Plan your trip carefully. Know the lay of the land, the snow conditions, and weather you'll most likely encounter. A young man left Yosemite to take a solo trip of 50 miles into the back country. Since it was April, he took only klister wax. A storm that dumped three feet of new snow hit him at the higher elevations. He had no way of removing the klister. Fortunately he was in better physical shape than mental preparation, and by brute strength he clomped the last 20 miles in knee-deep snow with three inches of ice clogged on his ski bottoms. A less powerful skier might not have made it. All this could have been avoided by prior planning.

6. Choose equipment that won't self-destruct under constant demand and will perform to a standard to ensure safe negotiation of an icy chute or close-knit trees. With today's innovative methods of designing fiberglass skis,

strength can often be attained without sacrificing lightness. After careful research, we decided that we could get away with 47 mm-wide skis and 3-pin boots and bindings to ski 1250 kilometers across Ellesmere Island. They would provide the speed we required over a route chosen to avoid the harshest terrain. Just because you are in the mountains, don't assume you must use heavy, ponderous gear. Using this super light equipment, we were also able to do some of the finest downhill skiing I've ever encountered, on the mountains poking out of the ice cap.

7. Keep your trips exquisite in their simplicity. Every aspect of the endeavor, whether it is food, equipment, or choice of route, should be reduced to its lowest common denominator, thus lessening the number of things that can go wrong.

8. Be as self-sufficient as possible in order to limit dependence on others and on the fickleness of nature. For the High Arctic Expedition we elected to haul 240-pound sleds over the countryside in order to avoid the questionable dependability of bush pilots to resupply us or of pre-set food caches which might have been destroyed.

Conditioning

Many people are curious to know what kind of conditioning I do before demanding multi-week mountaineering expeditions. The answer is nothing special. I keep myself in generally good shape, and that is enough for expeditions. No matter how strong you are, an 80-pound pack is always terribly heavy! Further, if the expedition is of two to three months duration, you'll want to start in less than tip-top shape so you'll peak for the "summit" — just as you'd want to for your most important citizens' races late in the season.

Doug Wiens, who has shared many of these expeditions with me, has his own proven method of "training." I'll let him expound:

"It is obvious that ski expeditions are energy-demanding; what is not so obvious is how to train in order to have the most energy available when it is needed. The accepted method has been 'working-out': running, roller skiing, weights, Exer-genies, and other such futile exercise. These exercises demand energy which I feel is squan-

Sledding up through a crevasse. (Ned Gillette)

dered. Before an expedition you shouldn't waste energy, you should save it and store it; hence I've developed a method I call *Horizontal Training*. The basic rule is, 'Never stand when you can sit, never sit when you can lie.' With proper storage you will accumulate vast energy reserves which can burst forth for explosive and extended effort.

"Some have confused this with mere laziness — not true. This is an exacting training schedule which demands long-term commitment and discipline. Nine to ten hours of sleep are a must, especially sleeping through till late morning to avoid this energy-draining time. Frequent siestas are also beneficial. A unique diet is important so the energy can be efficiently stored and not leak out. The combination of beer and pizza has been found by much experimentation to contain the proper balance of nutrients to maximize the storage of energy! Bon appetit and good training!"

As you can see, it takes a strong constitution to make the first-string expedition team!

11

CITIZENS' RACING

Citizens' racing is the term used for cross-country competitions that are open to all comers, young and old, fast and slow. The granddaddy of all races is Sweden's 85 km Vasaloppet, which annually attracts about 10,000 starters. Olympic-level international competitors line up with Swedes who do no other racing during the year. The local baker may have a bet with his neighbor on who can ski the distance faster. With the clashing of skis and poles, skiers grunting, falling, and shouting, the start approximates a

Skiers off the mark at the Norwegian Birkebeiner race. (Bjorn Finstad)

The Canadian Marathon. (Peter Miller)

medieval battle. Sheer numbers force some competitors to wait half an hour to move onto the trail. Once on the trail, things smooth out as each person slides into an individual rhythm for multiple hours of kicking and gliding.

In North America our biggest race is the 55 km American Birkebeiner at Telemark Lodge, Wisconsin, where several thousand skiers pay good money as an entry fee to leave a nice warm bed at 5 a.m., attempt to force a predawn breakfast down into a butterfly-infested stomach, and hurl themselves against the first horrible hill of 400 vertical feet and the following battleground of grueling kilometers. Throughout the United States and Canada there are scores of smaller citizens' races during the winter.

The increasing popularity of ski racing in North America shouldn't surprise anyone who reflects on the growth of road races and marathons. Just as a jogger every so often runs under the watch with a bunch of friends, so you should approach casual citizens' racing. That there is more equipment involved, waxes to be tested and applied, and a course that demands more concentration and technique doesn't make it any more formal or intense. You can be as serious about it as you want to be. I continue skiing citizens' races because they keep me honest and continue to hone my technique. Three to six races each year give me a reason to stay in shape and to throw old racing rivalries into comic relief.

How to Get Started

To get started racing, you don't have to have lots of training, years of skiing experience, or perfect technique. Find out from your local X-C shop, touring center, ski club, or division of the U.S. Ski Association when the races are being held. Then just head down to the race, wax your skis, and get out there and go for it! (The racing will take care of itself; all you have to do is ski attentively.)

Lots of people get psyched out just by the term "race." Think of it instead as a long ski and a festive carnival atmosphere with friends you've probably trained with, will race against, and may soon drink beer with!

Lynne von Trapp, the wife of the owner of the Trapp Family Lodge, is a competent touring skier but not terribly competitive. With a little encouragement from Trapp instructors, she finally decided to enter the 60 km Vermont Marathon. I told her, "Just get in the race and concentrate on relaxing and skiing well." It turned out that she skied a personally satisfying race and, not surprisingly, will do it again.

Your attitude may well determine what kind of a race you have. Get uptight and too intense and you'll not only miss the fun but have poor results. Serious enjoyment is the key to success as a citizen racer. After all, you're probably racing on a day off.

Race Strategy

First of all, whatever race you're going to, get there early. Give yourself enough time to get to know the course (this will be your warm-up as well). Sniff around and try to get a feeling first for the more radical sections of the course — corkscrewing downhills, grain elevator uphills, the sudden skate turn. This will also give you a chance to check the consistency of the snow.

If you're skiing very far from your wax kit, better carry a small fanny pack with waxes, cork, and scraper for testing

Citizens' races are for everyone. (Peter Miller)

or adjustment. Double-check your equipment: 20 seconds before the start is no time to begin adjusting your pole strap.

Most citizens' races feature a mass start, sometimes much more of a delight for spectators than for the racer that gets caught in the maelstrom. The gun goes off and immediately there is weeping and wailing and moaning and thrashing of skis. How to protect yourself in the midst of this chaos? First stake out your territory in the starting line, placing your poles well to the side to discourage encroachers. Station yourself in the pack according to your ability: if you're a hotshot, get up front; if not, go for a more modest start to prevent being engulfed from the rear.

Technically speaking, almost anything goes. Skating across the starting field is sometimes faster, but if the pack is tight you risk instant ski entanglement; double-poling would probably be better. Run on your skis if you must — don't let yourself be pushed around, pulled down, or skewered. Go for it in the beginning; the masses will sort themselves out and less frantic rhythms will soon be established.

Keeping a good rhythm going will ensure a good race. Most citizen racers cannot go all out for even 10 kilometers. Instead, be clever. Should you be striding on this flat section, or double-poling? Can you cruise behind another skier, letting his rhythm smooth out your own and pull you up some hills, or if you've been doing this, is it time to cut the cord and make your move? Don't think frantically about speed. Strong, efficient skiing will be fast skiing. Think of speed not as pain, but as getting there easily. If you know the course, push hard before restful downhills.

A note on howling. International-class racer Audun Endestad trained and taught at the Trapp Family Lodge. Having once skied for the Howling Wolf Express ski club in California, Audun frequently resorted to howling during races and soon had others howling as well. It was found to be a wonderful way of staying mentally tough but relaxed during a race and led to some antic responses of spectators shouting encouragement. Not that you necessarily have to howl, but making a little noise of your own will keep you loose and on top of things.

Even more important than howling is feeding adequately, especially in longer races. Slow down enough at feeding stations so the liquid goes into your mouth and not elsewhere. Don't neglect the first couple of stations just because you're feeling strong — you'll pay for it later. Don't be bashful about getting enough to drink; you'll probably spill half of it anyway, and only one mouthful of an energy liquid every 5 kilometers is not going to be very helpful. Nor will the solid food that is occasionally offered. (One competitor in a recent marathon was presented with some prime rib at 35 kilometers!)

Not all the bumps and dips are in the race course. In a race of any length there are bound to be some highs and lows in your mind. Often in a long race of more than 50 km I'll go through several stages when I feel that I just cannot go on. My very worst point in a long race seems to be somewhere between 35 and 40 kms. Yet these depressions

Strongman Audun Endestad in the new quick and powerful racing style. (Peter Miller)

always pass, and I get my concentration and energy back in the next kilometer. Your body will go farther than you believe it will. It's often just a matter of relaxing your mind.

Undoubtedly there will be some sections of the course on which you wish you could relax your body as well. Perhaps your wax isn't working very well or the course is especially strenuous. This is the time to concentrate on technique. Slipping on an uphill? Perhaps you're not looking up the hill and have gotten hunched over too far. Feeling slow on the flats? Maybe your poling has gotten sluggish, causing your tempo to drop off. Attention to technique will get your mind off the strain and pain.

Technique

Racing technique is merely a faster version of your touring technique, with a few modifications. Skiing faster is important, but equally important is efficiency. You don't

have to ski too many races before you realize that good technique is the key to "free" minutes gained with no more energy expended, especially in races of 50 and 60 kilometers. The super-conditioned racer whose technique is not well developed will begin to thrash and bash during a race, losing ground to a less well conditioned skier whose technique is refined. Economy of movement that will enable us to ski fast without tiring is our goal.

The new racing technique: There is a different way of skiing for today's racing, reflecting subtle changes from the days of skiing on wooden racing skis (pre-1974) or from straight touring technique. These changes make a noticeable difference in speed but can be easily misunderstood.

This new racing technique has come from four improvements: (1) faster plastic ski bases; (2) improved waxing products and methods; (3) stiff cambered fiberglass racing skis; (4) better and firmer ski tracks. The result has been more speed, which demands changes in technique. With your skis running faster you must be on top of them all of

Racers of equal ability with individual styles: Lead skier Nancy Ingersoll shows a lower forward stance than Janet Kellum. (Peter Miller)

the time with your weight properly forward or they'll leave you behind. This means that you'll ski at a quicker tempo, your legs and arms turning over faster. In order to recover quicker, stand up straighter on your skis with less extension of arms and legs. Shorter strides mean more efficiency. All the excesses have been trimmed in the interest of speed.

I can remember watching Odd Martinsen, the fastest relay racer in the world, in the 1968 Olympics. All of us wondered how he skied so fast on such straight legs. Clearly he was ahead of his time (and over his skis).

The old style that most of us used then may be nearly as fast, but it takes more out of you by demanding a body position that is lower and more extended, thus putting more strain on your legs and increasing recovery time, which slows your tempo. The new style allows you to go faster for longer. Once you get moving fast, if you ski with a high tempo and fast turnover it takes little to keep your inertia up. Before getting into it, here are a couple of cautionary notes: (1) Don't go right out and try to ski super fast with this new technique. Master it, then begin skiing certain sections of trail very fast until you can ski consistently fast and efficiently. (2) Don't try to ski like any particular racer. Different body builds result in different styles. One skier's uphill technique may be based on very strong arms. Without a similar set of "guns," you might find that technique exhausting. Analyze basic racing technique, then adapt it to your body build, ability, and conditioning. Remember that top international competitors are unbelievably strong and coordinated. Most of us mortals will have to gear down a notch or two from their style.

How to get into the right body position: To find the fast skiing position that is right for you, assume a static striding position (as if the camera caught you in midstride with your left arm and right leg forward). Stand on an absolutely straight knee — that will probably feel pretty awkward, as it blocks your hips, stiffens your body, and provides no power. Now bend your knee and sink down until you feel your thigh muscles begin to burn. This leaves you too far back on your ski. Now stand up straight again and push your knee forward, bringing you out onto your ski and aligning your hip over your foot. You must experiment to feel the subtle flex that provides speed, power, and efficiency. It should feel like a proper yoga position with aligned bones taking strains off muscles. Dynamically, to make this position work for you, you're shoving your knee forward as you ski, bringing the whole package with you (your hips and torso). It feels almost as if you're in a sort of body cast or that your upper body is fused to your knee. That is to say, *relatively* straight legs move your body *with* your legs so that you're working with your weight on top of the ski all the time.

Weight on the ski gives you a natural, powerful compression (kick) which is not to be misinterpreted as excessive bobbing up and down. Remember that your energy should be focused into sending you forward down the track.

Russia's Jevgeni Beljajev runs uphill in the World Championships. (Michael Brady)

Uphills: If you try this new body position on the uphills you'll find it puts your weight too far forward of your wax, making a slip more likely. On hills, get your foot somewhat out in front of your knee (it's as if you're pushing your heel forward), then roll up and over it. This puts more weight on your wax for a longer period of time. Obviously if you do this on the flat you'll be thrown way back on your ski and have little forward drive. Try it yourself for proof. To keep your body in the right position, look up the hill. Tired citizen racers often drop their heads, hinge forward at the waist, and find their skis are suddenly slippery.

On an early spring day I was out jogging on a snowy road. It was pretty slippery. I had to adjust my running style and my weight placement over my feet to get traction. I had to be delicate on my feet, almost pussyfooting along. I was struck by how similar this was to skiing uphill when wax is wearing off and skis are starting to slip or skiing in tracks that are filling with soft snow shearing away from the hard track underneath when you put pressure on it.

The skier must go uphill in these conditions on "little cat feet," not trying too hard, making subtle adjustments in body position, length of stride, and kick.

As much attention ought to be paid to your arms as to your body position and knee drive. Your arms ought to be crisply driving forward, lifting you up the hill like a high-jumper approaching the bar. There should be plenty of shoulder in your poling to bring your torso forward and give you increased leverage. On uphills, because of the slower speed, the arm stops at your hip to give maximum push and allow quick recovery to keep up your momentum. (This, incidentally, is true for your legs as well. If you overextend, it will take longer to bring your leg back through, thus slowing your tempo.) Your arms set your tempo; if they move quickly, your legs will follow. Tired racers pole sluggishly, letting their elbows come out from their bodies, thus losing power. Remember that the arm extension in poling is like a push-up, and push-ups are harder if your hands are way out to the side.

A running herringbone. (Peter Miller)

Technique for uphill herringboning is much the same in racing and in touring, but you think about it differently while racing. Concentrate on driving the leg straight up the hill instead of to the side. Step way forward each time. Drive your knees forward while your legs and skis are cocked out to the side. Your skis should not be radically

Power through double-poling with quick compressions. (Peter Miller)

"V"ed out. For quickness you should use as shallow a "V" as you can get away with.

Double-poling: The same excesses and overextension trimmed from your diagonal stride should be eliminated from your double-poling, because, with the newer, faster skis and firm tracks, double-poling is used more often than ever before. If your arms are strong enough, double-poling is often fastest and can be used in many sections of the course which heretofore demanded diagonal technique, even gradual uphills or fast tracks. Double-pole with arms that are slightly bent for maximum thrusting power. Compress onto the poles with a *sharp* downward action of the upper body. Concentrate on poling with a rapid tempo in order to maintain speed. When your arms have straightened out at the completion of your poling, don't continue to let them drift out and up behind you. If you do, you will be that much slower bringing them through for another stroke.

Tempo and Terrain

Seasoned racers continuously use terrain to their advantage. For skiing in slow snow and difficult terrain, use a quicker tempo to maintain momentum. Be an opportunist. For example, don't get stuck in the trough between a

Add a kick to the double-pole to maintain speed. (Peter Miller)

downhill and an uphill, but take some short, quick double-poles to carry your speed as far up the other side as you can, then use quick hands in diagonal striding to scamper up the rest of the way. Use a low tuck on downhills for maximum speed.

Training

You'll feel better racing in February if you've done some training in September or earlier. Again, training doesn't have to be super-serious business. If you're getting into citizens' racing, you're probably already a jogger or road runner, cyclist or hiker. The thing to do is to build on your already developed cardiovascular fitness while adding some specificity; that is, activities that most closely resemble skiing movements.

Why be specific? If you start skiing in early November having spent the summer running, you'll quickly find the small of your back and abdominal muscles strained and throbbing and your arms devastated. Clearly some upper body work should have been introduced into your training by early fall. The transition from skiing to running in the spring, with consequent aching Achilles tendon and tight calves and hamstrings, should remind you that skiing has used different muscles.

While running gives a strong foundation of fitness, some modifications are necessary. Vigorous uphill hiking, driving the knee forward and extending the rear foot behind, coupled with aggressive arm swing is a better approximation of the demands you'll put on muscles when you ski. Add your poles to this and the effect will be even better. Not only will you strengthen your arms, but with a little concentration and coaching from a friend you can eliminate technical errors as well, such as levering your elbow back instead of driving your hand down and back past your hip. Take your ski poles on a hike, using them on unbroken

Tuck for speed. (Peter Miller)

Roller skiing simulates snow skiing. (Frits Solvang)

uphills. Ski bounding with poles, in which you're vaulting and bounding on hills that approximate what you'd run up against in a race, will produce tremendous power and quickness; try intervals of 30, 60, and 90 seconds. Be especially careful to take a warm-up run first.

You'll see an increasing number of people out on the road on roller skis. Roller skiing is not for everyone, and I personally prefer running, but its value is considerable — it's the most frequently used exercise by skiers on the National Team. Double-poling on roller skis will make everyone stronger in the upper body. But unless you have a basically correct stride or can get some coaching, diagonal striding will maintain your on-snow mistakes. If you do roller ski, don't just stick to long-distance slow-tempo workouts. Vary your speed as you would have to in any ski race.

This so-called speed play is vital to any kind of training, particularly in the fall. I run easy distance in the summer, then sprinkle it with speed play in September and October, letting the terrain dictate the tempo — hard on the uphills, easy on the downhills, with some bursts of speed on the flat. This is most pleasant in the woods, running on the trails you'll be skiing on later. It's a more nimble kind of workout and a welcome relief from the monotonous accumulation of miles. This is my favorite kind of training, especially on a brilliant fall day. It is the best kind of training if you have limited time.

Skiing demands strong back, stomach, and arm muscles. Back lifts, sit-ups, pulling arm bands or Exer-genie and working on a roller board are all effective. Do your exercises no more than three times a week in sets of ten and gradually add resistance. Through repetitive sets you build up your mind's ability to handle stress and your muscles' ability to keep working after they are tired. Strength work is especially important for women since they usually have not been encouraged to develop large muscle groups.

Remember through all of this not to burn yourself out by pushing too hard or by being obsessive. Generally I train at two-thirds racing speed or below for more enjoyment and to prevent injuries. I listen to my body tell me what it needs and when to rest.

Roller skiing provides excellent arm strength training. (Frits Solvang)

Rest is one of the least understood parts of training. It is very important to rebuild the muscles that are stressed during training and racing. One day per week of rest is essential, and more if you feel you need it.

Remember that the important races are in February and March. Be careful not to overtrain, peak in the late fall or early winter, then ski poorly during the crux of the season. I'd rather train just enough to keep a fresh attitude than be stale from too many hours of intense heavy-duty training. I have discovered yoga, which is fantastic for flexibility and loose strength. My routine takes only 10 to 15 minutes each morning and I'm addicted to it. A top-flight competitor like U.S. team member Stan Dunklee will stretch for as much as an hour a day during the peak of his racing schedule.

My training has always been strongly influenced by the seasons and what is going on around me. For instance, woodcutting and gathering in the fall is productive in more than one way. This is a natural approach to training. Training should be fun — a bright spot in your day — as well as a way to relieve tensions. You need a year-round plan that fits your own life style, and a progression of intensity as you near the peak racing season. Remember to continue your training during the winter racing season. A race now and then isn't enough to maintain top form, although it will take the place of speed workouts in your regular training.

I skied for John Caldwell for a few years when he was coach of the U.S. National X-C Team. At that time, I'm afraid, I was a bit too young and much too intense to appreciate fully Caldwell's relaxed method of training. All the variation and lightness just didn't make sense. What I failed to see until recently was that training must be enjoyable, challenging, and varied — not just serious, repetitious routine.

Equipment has changed a lot since these skis. (Ned Gillette)

12 EQUIPMENT

We all know what happens when a certain number of monkeys get unlimited access to a certain number of typewriters. Trapp ski school instructors have access to equipment from all major manufacturers and ski on this gear in their characteristically intense, playful, but analytical fashion. What you get is not Shakespeare but some pretty strong opinions — and some resident confusion — on cross-country gear. It is astonishing how long it takes even experienced skiers to evaluate equipment and find the gear that best enhances their style and level of

Choose the equipment that matches your skiing activity. (Ned Gillette)

skiing. Most troubled of all is Trapp's 6-foot-6-inch black-bearded rental czar. He suffers patiently the equipment complaints of visiting skiers, but when his own equipment fails his wrath is thunderous, and co-workers and sales representatives alike seek either immediate solutions or protective shelter. All of which makes me sweat heavily in anticipation of writing a chapter on equipment.

If I were to go into equipment thoroughly enough to satisfy the inquisitive eagle-eyed technician, this book would have been delayed a year, and by now the chapter would be obsolete anyway. The best thing I can do is give you some suggestions on how to nose out good equipment. Most important, be willing to bend the ear (and flex the ski) of an experienced cross-country ski instructor in an expansive mood. I cannot emphasize this strongly enough: it is only by practical on-snow experience with equipment that you'll find what is right for you. Season after season at Trapp's we're reminded that cheap, poorly designed equipment can make skiing quite frankly unpleasant.

As a buyer, you should be interested in two things: performance and durability. You are a skier, not a scientist. Don't get caught up in asking picky technical questions. It really doesn't matter to you what the chemical make-up of P-Tex 2000 is. It *does* matter how it will perform and how long it will last — characteristics which count out on the trail.

Many folks want one ski or boot that will be suitable for racing as well as mountaineering. This simply isn't possible. If you can afford only one set, get what is appropriate for the toughest skiing in which you plan to participate. In all probability you'll find the sport enjoyable enough to buy a second, more specialized, pair later in your career.

Whether you are a beginning skier or a citizens' racer, here a few guidelines to follow so that you will have a reasonable background from which to ask questions and choose equipment that is right for your needs.

Skis

In choosing a pair of skis that is right for you, determine what your skiing style is, then match that style with the proper ski. Here are a few decisions to be made before you even walk into the shop:

A. What speed will you ski?
  1. Athletic (citizens' racer)
  2. Active (fast touring)
  3. Casual (slow ski walking)

B. How many times will you ski during the year?
  1. More than 15 times
  2. Less than 10-15 times

C. Where will you ski?
  1. In tracks
  2. Off-track

D. What is your downhill ability on X-C skis?
  1. Aggressive carved turns
  2. Slow skidded turns
  3. Prayer

E. What base do you want?
  1. Waxable for performance
  2. Waxless for convenience

F. What is cross-country skiing to you?
  1. Sport
  2. Recreation

As a general rule, if you answer number 1 to these questions (lower total score), you are a more aggressive skier and can handle skis that are higher in performance: narrower, lighter, stiffer cambered, with less sidecut, a softer and shorter tip, and less torsional stiffness in the tip. However, realize that the opposite criteria are what you look for for easy, cruising, forgiving skiing. (*Note:* In this test, many off-track skiers are "aggressive," so forgive this little inconsistency!!)

Bases — waxable or waxless: Your decision must be whether to go waxable or waxless. You can eliminate half the skis on the market by deciding whether you want the performance and adaptability of a waxable ski or the convenience of a waxless ski. A waxless ski will seldom out-perform a well-waxed ski, but it will always out-perform a poorly waxed ski. Two-wax systems on the market do simplify waxing, but if you view waxing as a hassle, don't hesitate to go waxless. Keep things in perspective: it's more important to be out there skiing than to be skiing on any particular type of ski.

The base material of a ski should be durable, reasonably fast, able to hold grip and glide wax, and easily repaired and maintained. As a tourist you should get a base that demands little day-to-day care; leave the sophisticated bases that require lots of preparation to the racers.

The following information concentrates chiefly on the pros and cons of waxless skis, not because I'm pushing you in that direction (quite the contrary, actually) but because I think you need a thorough understanding of the waxless concept before making a decision on which way to go. There is no better feeling in the world than speeding down a well-prepared trail on skis that are perfectly waxed. A waxless ski will never provide that feeling. You just have to determine if performance is worth learning how to wax. For me it certainly has been. With this, let's move on to waxless skis, but be assured that more on waxable skis will be found in the chapter on waxing.

I think 50 percent of the skiers in this country ought to be using waxless skis, but I also think everyone ought to know what is gained or lost by going waxless. Mike Brady, who brought a lot of the European knowledge of cross-country skiing to this country, states the case this way:

If you find waxing a hassle, go waxless. (Ned Gillette)

"When waxable skis are easy to wax — say in powder or spring snow — waxless skis have no advantage. Only when it's difficult to wax skis, such as in transition conditions (32°F./0°C.), do waxless skis have any measurable advantage." Waxless skis have been used successfully in international racing to overcome difficult waxing problems. Bill Koch had the third fastest leg in the 1976 Olympic relay, and Norway's Per Knut Aaland won a silver medal in the 1979 Holmenkollen 50 km. Is this a hint of things to come?

Although many waxless skis are effective in certain conditions don't expect miracles from them. Their base

In waxless skis, choose hairy, bumpy, or smooth bases. (Peter Miller)

designs offer only one solution for a variety of snow conditions which you will meet out on the trail during your skiing career. As Harold Bjerke of Swix Sport International (a major wax manufacturer) says, "Just remember that using a waxless ski is like playing 18 holes of golf with only the putter."

Besides the sacrifice of performance to convenience, another trade-off with waxless skis involves time: while you save waxing time, you usually have to work harder. Waxless skis are usually a bit draggy, so you have to use more effort to push them forward. And they often backslip on hills, so you have to sweat to get to the crest.

For the right people, waxless skis are great. My mother got into cross-country about 10 years ago when she quit

Alpine skiing. She found at first that she didn't ski as much as she would have liked to; waxing was a hassle for her. A new pair of waxless skis solved the problem, and now she skis twice as often. I own a couple of pairs which I use when the waxing conditions are difficult, or when I have only a few minutes to ski.

Waxless skis are also the logical choice for people who shuffle only a few miles, for occasional skiers who want convenience, for those who ski in areas like the Northwest and California with lots of 32°F./0°C. weather and rapidly changing snow conditions, and for enthusiasts who ski well but want a third pair of skis for transitional snow. They're good, too, for kids who are just beginning to ski, but be careful not to buy a child's ski that has too long a waxless pattern — if the child isn't heavy enough, the ski won't slide downhill.

There are so many waxless skis on the market today that I find it more confusing to pick the best waxless concept than to select the right wax for the day. You name the geometric design, and manufacturers have tried it. In my opinion, the future will bring great strides forward in waxless skis that are smooth-bottomed and don't wear out, have good glide, turn easily downhill, have base "patterns" similar to the average size of snow crystals, and can vary somewhat to snow hardness and moisture content — in other words, similar to waxable performance. This ski is still in the lab.

It's not simply the *kind* of waxless base put on by a manufacturer that makes a difference in performance but also the way in which it is *attached* to the ski and the way in which the design and camber of the ski itself enhances the pattern. For instance, some factories put too much heat and pressure in their ski molds, resulting in a flattening of the pattern and little on-snow grip. Further, take different brands of mohair skis: some work, others are disasters; it makes a tremendous difference where the mohair strip is placed, how long it is, how far the hairs stick out, how stiff the hairs are, and what kind of glue is used. Steps, scales, rounds, diamonds, crowns, and smooth bases all vary among manufacturers. To choose a good waxless ski is tricky; my advice is to try out as many types as you can from rental programs, ski in the typical snow condition of your area, then obtain the help of a good salesperson to make your final decision.

Waxless skis are usually used by folks whose main problem is getting up hills. Choose a ski that has good gripping capability and a soft enough camber so the grip section of the ski will firmly contact the snow. Remember that patterns on the bases of skis make a ski somewhat harder to turn downhill. So don't fail to include some downhill runs in your testing. (A while ago a major ski manufacturer introduced a waxless pattern that resisted even the experts' efforts to turn it right or left.) A final note: waxless skis are usually sold to people who just want something to get around on. Regrettably, there are many skis on the market which make it impossible to do just that. Take the time to find a ski that will really work for you.

Waxless skis are not maintenance-free. For best performance (although not essential) the tips and tails of polyethylene-based skis should be prepped with glider wax to enhance the glide. Some wax companies are offering special spray glider waxes for increased speed of waxless skis in dry and wet snow conditions. Silicone speed spray will help prevent the frustrating tendency of some waxless skis to collect ice in the pattern or between the hairs at the freezing point. In spring conditions, waxless patterns will pick up old klister wax and crud along the trail, making for a sluggish ski. Liquid wax remover rubbed on with a rag will cure this problem.

One wax company is even planning to market a waxless grip wax to enhance the grip of waxless skis in special snow conditions and as the base pattern wears out. If they're not careful, they'll invent wax all over again!

Length: The old rule of measuring a ski to the wrist of your outstretched arm still holds true in cross-country. A longer ski will be faster and more stable but less maneuverable. I wouldn't go any shorter than 10 cm from your normal length to try for more maneuverability. And don't go shorter than normal length if you plan to race — you'll need the speed and stability.

Width: Wider skis are more stable, stronger, and provide more flotation in deep snow but are slower in tracks.

Weight: Lighter means faster in tracks. Heavy skis don't necessarily mean stronger skis. Light equipment

Olympic medal winner Bill Koch double-checks his skis before racing. (Ned Gillette)

allows you to ski with more sensitivity than does heavier gear; when you do something right or wrong, you feel it right away. For long tours and heavy packs you usually need sturdy equipment (although we skied 1250 km in the Arctic on skis 47 mm wide!). But for track skiing at touring centers, don't overlook the fact that your technique is to a large extent a result of your equipment. You are what you ski on. Those of you who jog know that running with light shoes allows you to go faster, longer, and more easily. A bit of speed over the snow will put X-C into an entirely different perspective.

Tip flex: To feel this in the shop, simply pull the tip toward you with one hand while feeling the stiffness and transition into the body of the ski with the other hand flat on the ski. Softer tips are faster in machine-set tracks. Stiffer tips are more stable for touring and for holding downhill turns off-track. A longer tip coming farther down into the body of the ski is better for touring and more forgiving since it follows the terrain more easily; shorter tips are better for forceful racing.

Tip splay: Squeeze the skis together. If the tips splay apart down into the body of the skis, they will not track well or turn easily because you are actually skiing on less than the functional part of the ski; guaranteeing a squirrelly ride down any hill.

Torsional stiffness: Twist the ski tip left or right as if you were trying to unscrew the tip from the ski. Stiffer tips

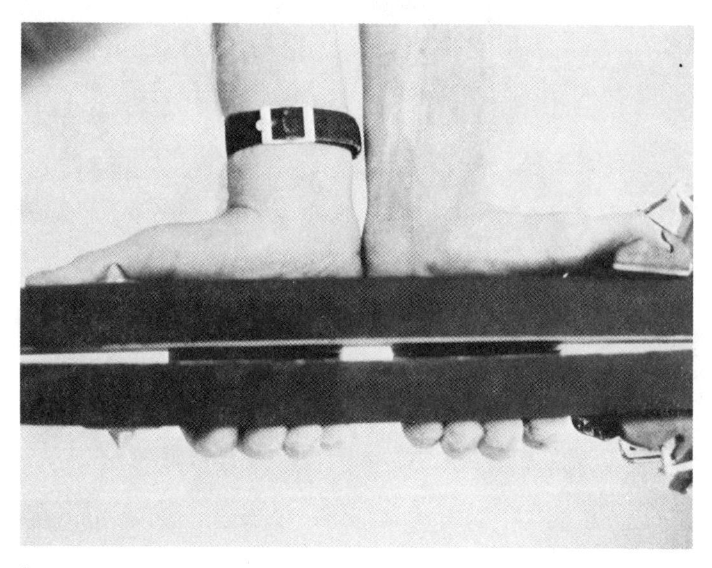

Some racing skis are so stiff in the middle you cannot press them together. (Ned Gillette)

give better edge-holding ability for touring, especially on hard-packed snow, while softer tips are better in tracks because they tend not to catch on the sidewalls and ride out of the track.

Camber: Camber is the arch of a ski that distributes your weight over the running surface. When skis are placed bottom to bottom and pressed together, a soft pair will be easy to press together, a stiff pair quite difficult. Each length of ski is given a camber stiffness that is correct for the average weight of a skier who would use that length. For instance, most 210 cm skis are cambered for 165 to 175 pounds, the average weight of a 5-foot-11-inch male human. But all pairs within a given length of one brand vary a bit, and brands themselves vary, so if you are light for your height, you should choose a ski with softer camber. Occasionally you must go to a shorter ski to get a softer one.

Racers prefer stiffly cambered skis. They're faster because the new pressure distribution patterns keep the base's waxed center section, by and large, up off the snow when the skis are equally weighted, as on downhills and flat stretches of double-poling. When the racer kicks and presses down on one ski, the center portion of the base is

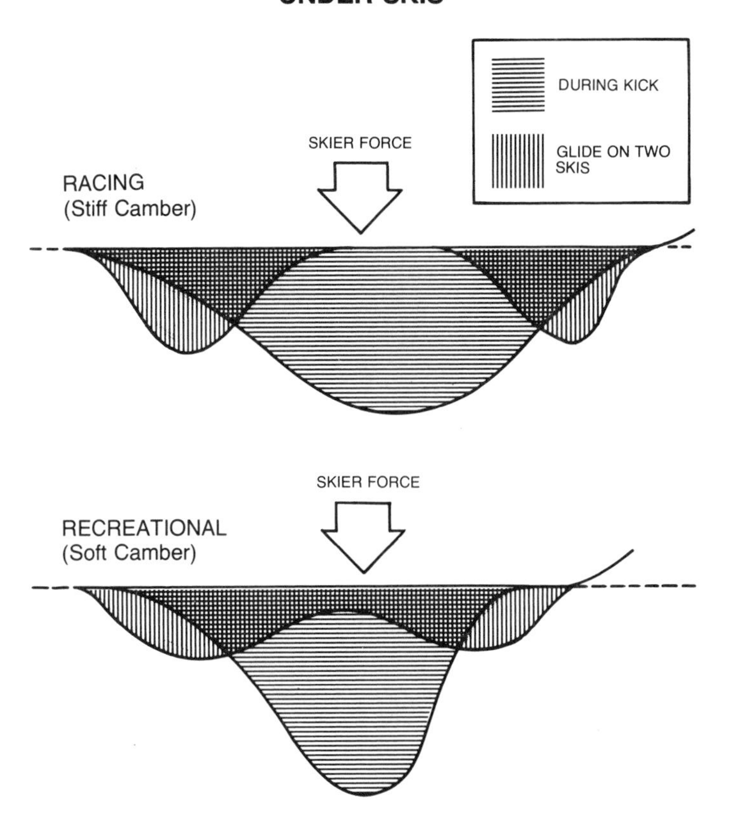

pressed onto the snow, providing grip. These skis demand an energetic kicking action on well-prepared tracks. (Super-stiff skis are used in klister conditions, softer skis in powder snow.) Stiffer skis also provide positive edge control but demand an expert skier to make them turn.

Softer skis are more forgiving since they are easier to flatten, thus allowing the wax or waxless pattern to bite readily into the snow for uphill grip. They provide better grip for off-track cruising in deep snow and are more easily turned in slow-speed skiing. If I had a choice, I would buy a ski that is a little too soft rather than too stiff. A softer ski may be a little slower, but at least you can make it up the hills with ease.

Sidecut: Many X-C skis are designed to be wider at the tip and tail than at the center. This is called sidecut. You can identify it by placing the sidewalls of the skis together and determining how much space is between skis in the midsection. A light touring ski usually has 2-7 mm of sidecut, while a touring ski is cut with 5-10 mm. A ski must have adequate torsional stiffness in the tip to utilize sidecut.

It is assumed that more sidecut (within limits) means the ski will track better and wander less when used in nontrack skiing. Sidecut also helps in holding a turn (bringing you around) and in providing stability at higher speeds. Less sidecut is faster in race tracks (less drag of the tail flaring). It is better in slow pivoting turns because it starts the turn more easily, but it doesn't hold as well during the turn.

Frankly, the verdict on sidecut isn't in. But generally speaking you'll find touring skis with sidecut and racing or light training skis with little or none.

Matched pair: Squeeze the skis together and sight down the closing line. Do they close at the same rate? Is there a hard spot in one? Are they compatible?

Of course no one characteristic makes a ski. Everything must work together to produce a ski which will perform for your intended use and proficiency as a skier. Try to get the skis out on the snow (demo skis from rental programs are your best bet) to find out for yourself. If you've skied on a friend's skis that seem to have the right camber for you, take them along when shopping. Check cambers by pressing together one of the friend's skis and one of those you're considering buying.

Repairs you can do yourself: 1. Gouges in bases: Sharp rocks can cause deep scars in the base of your polyethylene skis. To repair, dry the base and clean all old wax and grit from the area to be repaired. Trim away any flaps of base material hanging from the wound. Light the end of a P-tex candle and allow it to drip on a fireproof surface until the drippings are soot-free. Hold the candle about ¼ inch above the base of the ski and fill the scratches. After the patch has cooled and hardened, use a metal scraper to take off the excess. Do final smoothing with fine sandpaper or steel wool.

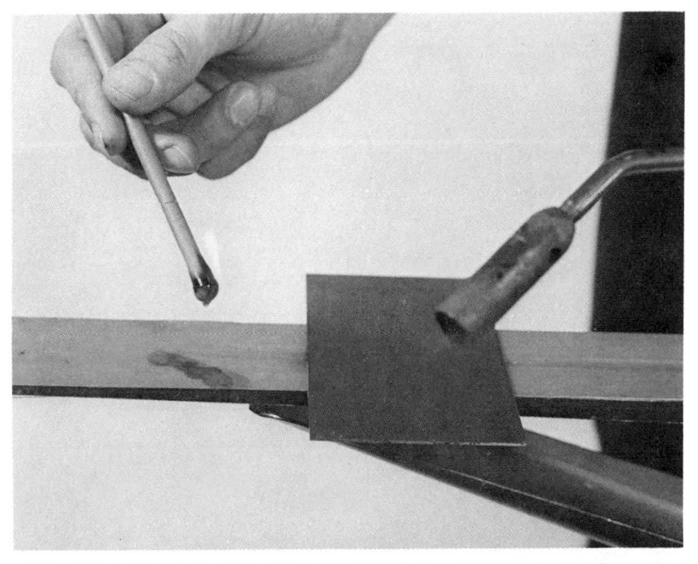

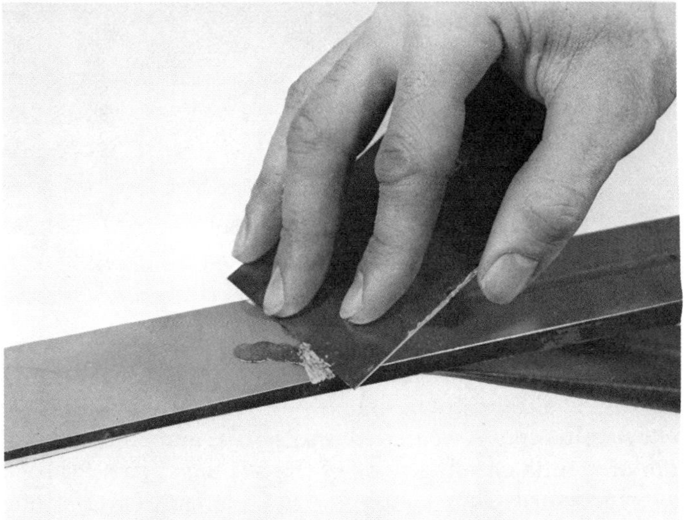

Filling and smoothing gouges in bases. (Peter Miller)

2. Cracks in sidewalls: Use epoxy glue to seal the opening and prevent water seeping into the core. This is not a structural failure.

3. Loose binding screws: These can occur if holes are originally drilled too large. Simply plug the holes with steel wool mixed with epoxy, then put the screws back in.

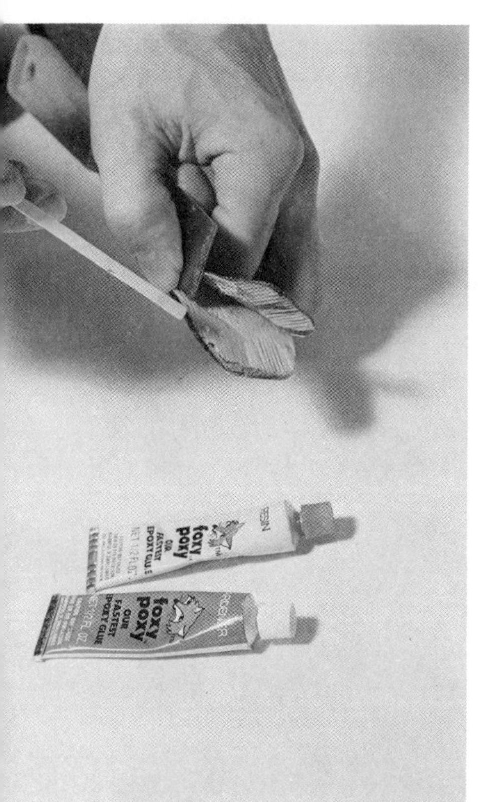

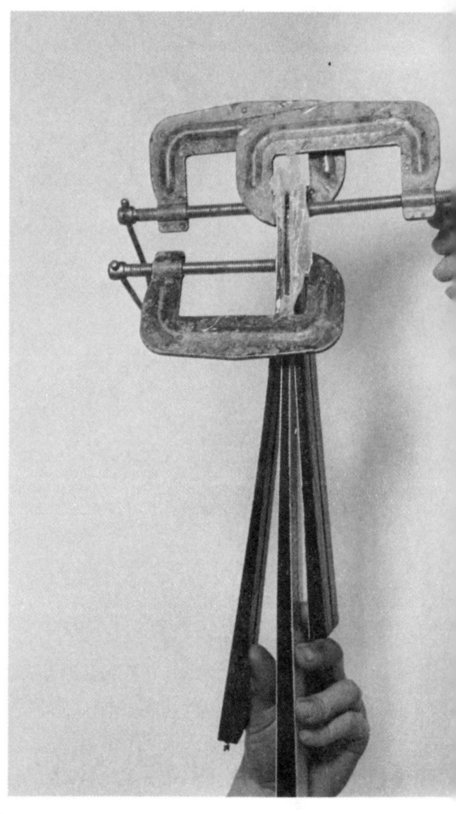

Delaminations can be glued and splinted. (Peter Miller)

4. Delamination: Carefully clean the damaged area and pry open as far as possible. Spread epoxy over the surfaces, pushing it as far into the delamination as possible. Squeeze out surplus epoxy, wrap with wax paper, and place wood or metal splints on either side of the ski to act as a form for even pressure. Clamp snugly with C clamps, being careful not to press all the glue out.

Summer Storage: Give your skis a coat of glider wax on the full length of the base and leave it unscraped. Then just set them against the wall in a relatively cool, dry room.

Boots

Cold, wet, and sore feet make cross-country skiing pretty unpleasant, so if you're on a budget, spend your money on high-quality boots and skimp a bit on other items of equipment. You get what you pay for in performance and durability.

Quality boots for cross-country are flexible fore and aft for ease of striding and climbing, but torsionally rigid to resist twisting off the ski when turning downhills, thereby providing maximum control. So a good boot is both flexible and rigid, seemingly contradictory characteristics which are built into top-line boots only. Stitched sole boots will provide the maximum lateral stability, but they are expensive. Some of the high-topped, thick-soled kinds are also rigid if they have a stout wood or metal shank under the instep, but check them out carefully by twisting the sole in your hands before buying them. Downhill gives people the most problems in cross-country skiing, and most of them come from wearing cheap boots with flimsy soles which allow your heel to slide off the ski as you initiate a turn, thus canceling any direct transferral of steering

Alpine, general touring, light touring, and the new racing boots. (Peter Miller)

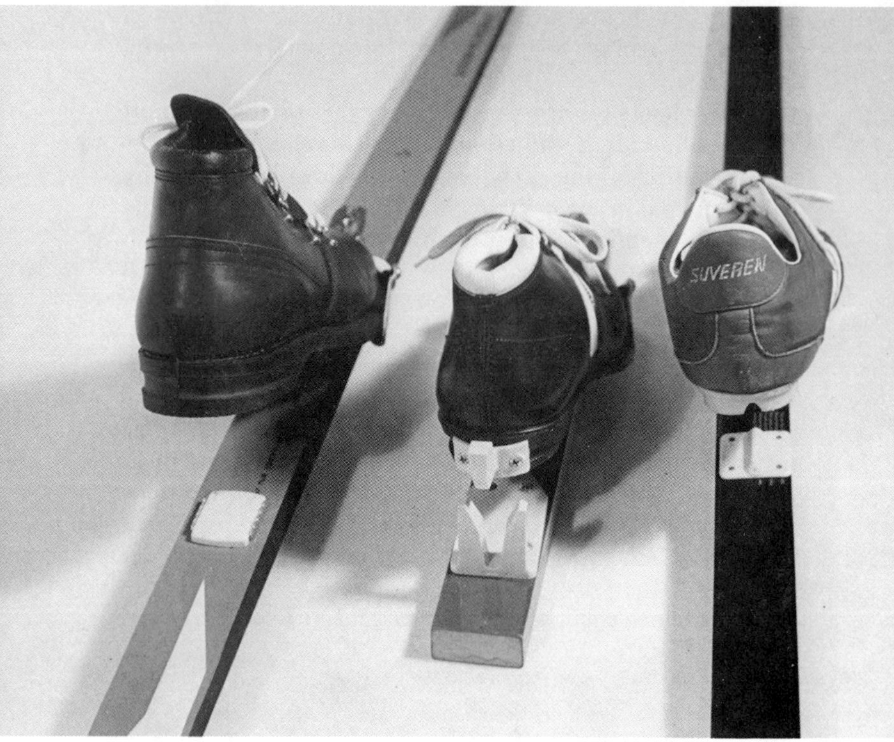

Teeth, "V"s, and ridges help keep your heel on the ski. (Peter Miller)

power from your legs to your skis. There are special heel devices on the market which allow free heel lift for flat striding while laterally locking your heel into a "V" for downhill sections. They are simple and very effective but can't rescue an insubstantial boot.

Double-check that the boot is the 75 mm Nordic or accepted racing norm, that the sole is securely attached to the upper, and that the pin plate at the toe is well fastened into the sole.

Full-grain leather costs more but is warmer, more water resistant, more comfortable, and more durable while retaining its breathability so foot perspiration can escape. Several synthetics, both waterproof and porous, are on the market as well.

The ideal fit is similar to a comfortable street shoe you wouldn't mind walking in for several miles. This requires a snug fit at the heel and instep with plenty of width for toes to wiggle freely for warmth. When the boot is flexed forward it should not crease painfully across the toes; small creases are more comfortable. A proper insole will be warm, durable, and moisture absorbent. Make sure the heel counter is durable and comfortable. Fleece-lined boots look warmer, but an extra-light pair of socks will do the same job in an unlined boot, and the boot will dry out faster.

The 75 mm boots are the old standby for all-purpose skiing, wilderness touring, and 3-pin downhill skiing. The new nylon-soled racing boots provide more freedom of movement on the flat and increased downhill control compared to the older 75 mm boots. There's not a Trapp instructor who wears the old-style boots anymore (we do mainly track skiing), but you can get an argument on which brand is best. Besides foot fit, the main point of discussion is how tightly the boot engages the binding and how quickly the nylon sole wears down and fatigues, causing loss of downhill control. For a test of durability, we used 50 mm high-topped racing boots for the skiing portion of our circumnavigation of Mt. McKinley. They held up well, even under the stress of carrying 80-pound backpacks. But I wouldn't recommend them for this use!

Remember that the new racing boots are a specialized design for a specialized purpose — fast skiing in tracks. They're inadequate for walking any distance on a road at the end of a tour and downright dangerous if you have to do any scrambling over rock. Also, they're generally not as warm or watertight as heavier 75 mm boots, although an overboot is an easy solution. Consider the innovations in downhill boots and binding and in running shoes in the last five years. My guess is that similar advances in cross-country footwear are on the way.

Bindings

Here we're talking about the touring and racing variety. For most cross-country skiing all you need is a toe binding, and by now it's pretty hard to find a truly bad 75 mm. If you're after the newer rigs and choose one of the 50 mm variety, you'll find a number of compatible bindings from different manufacturers. The technology is still new and a mouse could venture into some with utter impunity. Other manufacturers offer a binding that fits only the boot they make.

Poles

Poles are often overlooked, but they are a functional part of your skiing. Many beginners feel awkward with their poles because they've gotten them too long or too short or with straps that can't be properly adjusted. The right pole will help you ski better and provide a good percentage of your power instead of merely the balance of outriggers. Proper length should bring the top of the pole snugly up under your armpit as it stands on a hard floor.

You'll want a solid, wide basket for touring so it doesn't sink into the snow too much (although it will tend to lever the pole out on steep slopes) and a rugged stainless steel tip

Baskets are a designer's delight. (Peter Miller)

at the base. The new hoof-shaped racing baskets are good for just that — racing or fast track skiing. But try to use them for downhill checking or support for a kick turn on steep slopes and you'll find them skittering over the snow instead of sticking in. The shaft can be of tonkin cane, aluminum, or fiberglass. Whatever the material you choose, make sure it provides strength, rigidity, and a good swing weight. The technology of racing poles is now sufficient to keep an equipment-obsessive entranced for days.

Backpacks for Skiing

Skiing with a pack is never as pleasant as skiing free, but for all-day tours it is necessary to bring along extra clothing, waxes, map, sunglasses, and a few things to eat; as well as a spare tip in case of a broken ski, space blanket and matches for emergencies. Include tape — adhesive tape for blisters and strapping tape for repairing broken equipment. Tape is an instant all-inclusive repair kit. (People have even been known to tape bindings back onto skis!)

A good-sized fanny pack may well be all you need for fast tours close to home, since it hinders skiing movement very little. But for ventures further afield, you'll want a bit more capacity. I prefer a day pack that is fairly tall but not too wide, so my arms can swing freely. I've found that most climbing rucksacks are a pretty good bet: they'll provide enough capacity so you don't have to cram everything in so tightly that you end up with a tight "ball" on your back, which is uncomfortable.

The problem on multi-day treks of course is how to carry all the gear and still enjoy the experience. The first step is to choose a larger pack that is comfortable, stable, and simply designed. I find that most designers get carried away with the process of designing and forget that serious backpackers want only what is necessary out on the trail. Remember that you'll be operating cords and buckles on the trail with cold hands or mittens. Intricate systems often let you down when you most need them. For control while touring, stay away from packs that roll with every skiing movement. Choose one of the specially designed soft packs or interior-frame packs which "cling" to your body. This is especially critical in downhill skiing situations where a loose pack will exaggerate any error you commit, often throwing you off balance and leading to bruising or dangerous falls. The totally soft packs are more stable but more difficult to pack. The manner in which they are packed forms the frame. Be careful not to have hard objects jabbing into your back. Consider packing a sweater along the back for padding.

I like soft packs best for medium-weight loads. For heavy and larger loads on extensive tours, I go with an interior-frame pack which helps to distribute the load more comfortably. Important for ease of carrying loads is a sophisticated yet simple arrangement by which an auxiliary strap "picks" the weight up off your shoulder straps, thereby lessening the pressure on your shoulders, especially while poling. (The trade-off here is that the pack tends to sway a bit more.) A sternum strap which links the two shoulder straps across the chest further frees shoulder movement and eliminates sway. Make sure all straps can be adjusted while you are skiing. A wide waist belt which is padded at the hips and easily closed by Velcro or quick-release buckle further fastens the pack so it almost becomes part of your body and moves with it.

Make sure that pockets are removable so you can use the pack for faster skiing and complete poling extension if you wish. Side straps which can be used to carry skis on your pack are useful in case you have to walk the last couple of miles of the tour. Compartmentalize your gear by packing certain similar things in nylon stuff sacks and labeling each. In this way you'll maintain some order when unpacking at your campsite. Pack heavy items low and closest to your back for maximum stability. Items needed during the day should be placed on top for easy access.

As you might suspect, to ski with a heavy backpack you'll have to make considerable adjustments in your technique. I recall starting off around Mt. McKinley with 80 pounds on our backs (our skis were only 47 mm wide and we used 3-pin bindings). At first I could barely support the load, to say nothing of moving forward or negotiating downhills. But we all adapted and somehow continued beyond the first tentative steps.

Heavy weight on back makes skier go splat. (Ned Gillette)

Weight on your back accentuates any mistake, so the key is not to make any mistakes. I ski very conservatively with a heavy pack, often electing to make a series of traverses down a slope rather than link turns. Unless I require additional pushing power uphill, I use my poles relatively little in comparison to skiing without a pack and keep my hands low as if I'm walking. Since packs press down on the muscles running across the top of the shoulders, raising the hands high in front brings fatigue faster. Falling with the persuasion of a big pack is never subtle. Try your utmost to maintain your balance, but when all is obviously lost, let go and relax, trying to avoid jamming head and shoulders into hard snow or rocks. Our McKinley trip very nearly had to be aborted after Allan dislocated a shoulder in a fall that was vicious only because of the weight he carried.

Sleds

During the High Arctic Expedition to Ellesmere Island each man hauled his gear in an 8-foot fiberglass sled. It was the only practical means of transporting 240 pounds apiece. We got the sleds through chaotic ocean pack ice, up steep glacier tongues, and down rocky river valleys. Of course you must choose your route carefully — certain terrain eliminates sled hauling — but consider a sled as a practical alternative to humping heavy backpacks. I prefer boat-type sleds which float on the snow and have angled sides to prevent capsizing in deep snow. Longer sleds tend to even out small terrain variations. Rigid fiberglass pulling poles control the sled effectively; some come equipped with springs at the junction to the waist belt for easier striding action. I prefer a chest-shoulder-and-waist-combination pulling harness.

Other uses for sleds are for toting the small kids on a tour or packing supplies into a hunting or fishing camp or off-the-road homestead.

Winter Photography

No matter if you're making a serious expedition or doing some day touring with friends, someone in the party will doubtless have a camera along. Winter photography is not quite as easy as summer shooting, so I'll offer a few hints to help you avoid some of the errors that I made while learning how to record the events on expeditions.

On our 1978 ski around Mt. McKinley, four photographers took 9,000 transparencies in a three-week period and brought back some great photographs. (We did more skiing and climbing than photographing although it doesn't sound like it.) National Geographic ended up using only eight in their magazine! You've got to shoot a lot to get good. I am purely a point-and-shoot man, proof that anyone who sets mind to it can become proficient.

You must be willing to work for good photos. Try to get different camera angles on your subject by lying on your stomach and shooting up, or hiking up a nearby hill and shooting down. Use your imagination! Don't be afraid to set up the scene. Vary your shots further by using different lenses. On expeditions when I'm severely limited by weight considerations I use a 28 mm and a 80-200 mm zoom as my standard lenses, each on a separate body. Two bodies are good insurance, plus you don't have to keep changing lenses in snowstorms.

Have your camera ready for use. That white-tail deer isn't going to wait around while you wrestle your camera

Arctic char dinner at Lake Hazen, Ellesmere Island. (Ned Gillette)

out of your backpack. Keeping your camera around your neck on one of the many special tight-fitting harnesses is the quickest. Since I can't stand to have my camera hanging about my neck, I wear a fanny pack backwards, which gives me reasonably fast access to my cameras. With this system I can still tote a backpack. Keep your camera shutter cocked at all times. Don't worry about the occasional wasted frame from accidentally tripping the release. Be ready to capture that once-in-a-lifetime shot.

Most people bring home photographs of the majestic landscape on a grand scale. I try to concentrate on close-up shots of what the people around me are going through on the trip, reactions to fatigue, danger, humor, bad wax, nasty weather, and each other. The photos that usually bring the house down during my adventure slide shows are rapid recording of the circumstances that brought the skier down: Galen's wildly processional, gravity-defying abandonment of anything that passes for downhill control on the McKinley expedition.

Exposure is tricky in the snow. You can pretty much trust your meter for the wide panorama shots. But if it's the person in your frame for which you want to expose correctly, you must be more clever. Get your reading by holding your meter up close to your subject's face, or take a reading off your own hand.

As a general rule, if you're shooting people, an exposure of f/5.6 at 1/500 second with ASA 25 film is always close in bright sunlight on snow. Bracketing, or taking pictures at one f/stop above and below the meter reading, is a good idea for important shots. Remember that the colors are richer and shadows longer early and late in the day. This is the time for those dramatic pictures. Midday light is deceptively flat.

Cold by itself does not harm equipment. Condensation on camera and lenses will be a problem only if you are constantly warming and cooling a camera: walking inside suddenly to a warm room, or placing the camera next to your body, then out in the cold for long periods. You have to make a decision to keep your camera either body temperature or outside temperature on multi-day ski trips. I choose to keep my Nikons cold and my small Rollei 35 warm in my pocket.

Cold hands are troublesome in winter shooting. With a lot of outdoor work, it is possible to toughen your hands somewhat so you can handle your cameras for long periods without gloves. Silk inner gloves are a good compromise. And you *can* get proficient enough with mittens to work a camera while keeping your hands toasty warm.

Kahiltna Glacier, Mt. McKinley. (Ned Gillette)

13
WAXING

Waxing may be a little more complicated than making a peanut butter and jelly sandwich, but the aim is to keep it simple. You can pretty much do what you want, imitating the racer's iridescent combination of klisters or making use of a less flamboyant two-wax system for touring. We've seen it all on the waxing benches at the Trapp Touring Center where "the wax of the day" is often pursued with near frenzy and the solutions would satisfy an abstract expressionist.

Why take the time and trouble to wax well? You'll have "fast" skis that glide easily. Many beginning and even intermediate skiers are fearful of speed. "I don't want a fast ski," they protest. But if they think of it as doing less work, their response will be quite different.

How Wax Works

Watching good cross-country skiers, you can hardly believe that one wax will allow a person to ski on the flat, uphill, and down with only a slight change in technique.

How is this possible? I turn to ski scientist Mike Brady, who has long been on intimate terms with ski waxes and ski bottoms: "A waxed ski behaves this way because small microscopic irregularities of the snow surface penetrate the wax just enough to allow a good grip when a ski is weighted, yet allow a moving ski to glide." If you use wax that is too soft, the snow particles will penetrate too far into the wax and you'll be able to walk up the side of a barn door, but you'll be so sticky that you'll have to walk down the other side as well. If you put wax on that is too hard, the snow particles cannot penetrate at all. Your skis will perform like an Alpine ski. They'll be like greased lightning on the downhills but in definite need of a mechanical lift on the uphills.

A day's skiing may require waxing changes. (Michael Brady)

Grip Waxes

These waxes give you purchase on the snow. (Speed waxes, to be covered later, provide faster glide.) They can be divided into three categories.

Hard wax is for snow that is in its original condition. It may have been on the ground for several days, but it still hasn't melted, refrozen, or otherwise changed.

Klister is tacky fluid, the consistency of toothpaste, for snow that has been through changes to form wet or icy conditions. It has melted, melted and refrozen, or melted, refrozen and melted several times. After all these changes the original prickly crystals have become so rounded off that they can't penetrate hard wax; hence oozy klister.

Klister-wax is halfway between hard wax and klister for use at temperatures around 32°F./0°C. (freezing). It's messy stuff and fortunately seldom used.

Ingredients: All waxes, both hard and klisters, share some common ingredients, although in different proportions depending on the type of snow for which they are intended (big wax firms no longer use beeswax, alas for the romantic legends of the past):

1. Petroleum wax for water repellency
2. Synthetic rubber for adhesion
3. Oil and vaseline to soften hard wax; synthetic resin to soften klister

I've had the curious experience of touring the catacombs of the Swix wax factory in Norway. There, in huge vats, are gallons and gallons of raw wax, bubbling and steaming and ready to be piped up to the cannister-filling machines. It made me wonder if any eye of newt, toe of frog, wool of bat, or tongue of dog had recently been added.

Selection: The cannisters and tubes which receive the molten wax are color-coded for easy selection. It pretty much follows the spectrum: colder colors for cold snow — green and blue; warmer colors for warmer snow — purple, red, and yellow. When Trapp instructors put a waxing suggestion on the blackboard, they haven't had to sacrifice a sheep or turn to a computer to get the wax of the day. They've simply checked the temperature on a thermometer located in the shade and determined whether the snow has been melted and refrozen (turning it into klister snow) and matched that with the directions on a cannister of wax. After a while you'll find that it becomes fairly routine: if the temperature is in the low twenties, red wax won't get a second glance.

Many people take the posted "wax of the day" as an article of faith. One Trapp instructor answered a telephone inquiry by saying, "Right now we're using special green." Several seconds passed, then a desperate and incredulous voice asked, "You mean it might change?" Change it may, and if you want to ski successfully you'll have to be willing to make some changes in your wax. With the wide changes of temperature in the Sierra, some days will call for a

WAX CHART

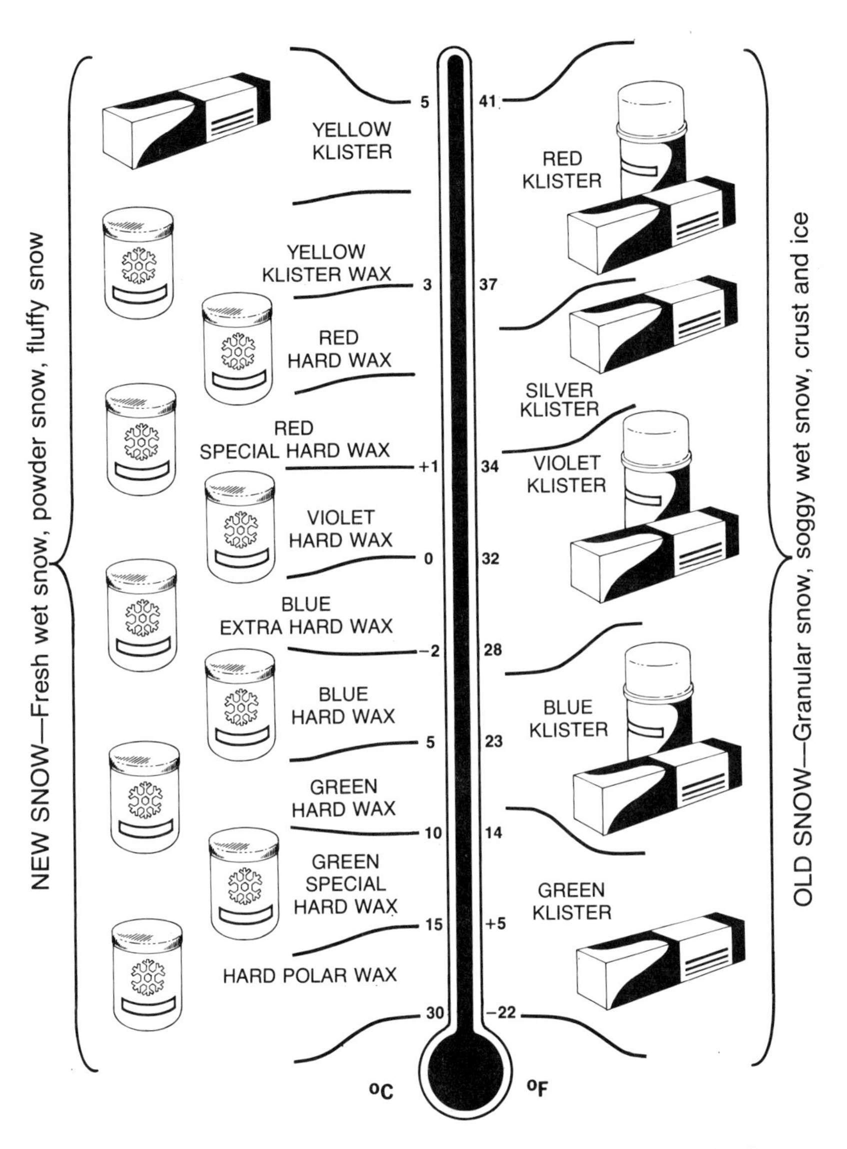

Information courtesy Swix Wax Company

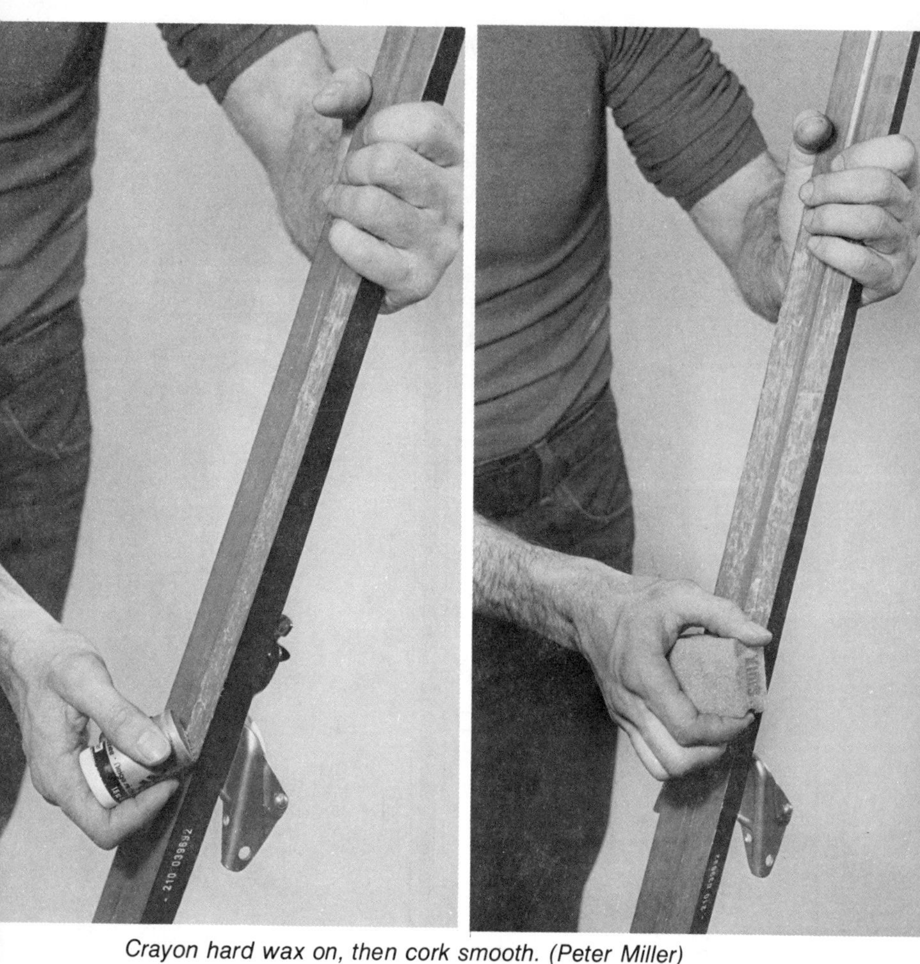

Crayon hard wax on, then cork smooth. (Peter Miller)

complete ransacking of the wax box; yet Alaskan skiers may cruise serenely on special green for days on end. Skiers leaving a touring center for a higher ridge may find that as the snow gets colder the higher they go, the purple wax that worked well for the first couple of kilometers has to be scraped off and replaced with blue.

Application: Most skiers, even beginners, won't have an especially hard time figuring out what wax to use. If in doubt you can always take a sly look about you to see what others are using. Problems occur putting the wax on the ski bottom. (One inquiring skier at Trapp's, complaining about slippery skis, was told to add a little purple underfoot. He sat down straightaway and waxed his shoes.) Although blue may be the right wax, it will be awfully slow if applied like stucco; likewise red klister if applied thickly enough to merit anchovies and mushrooms.

Hard wax is easy as long as your ski is dry (outside you may have to wipe the moisture off with a gloved hand or bandanna). Peel back the wax tin and simply rub it on as if you were coloring the base with a crayon. Using the edge of the wax results in a smoother layer. Rub the wax out with short vigorous strokes of a cork to make it faster and more durable.

Klister is rowdy stuff and will readily transfer itself to your hands, clothes, and hair if not kept on a short leash. Warm the tube slightly with a torch, near a fire, or in your hand to make it squeezable (you don't have to bring it to a rolling boil); cold klister is impossible to extract from the tube. Squeeze a thin ribbon down each side of the groove by pressing the nozzle flat against the ski bottom. Smooth it

Squeeze klister on, then spread evenly. (Peter Miller)

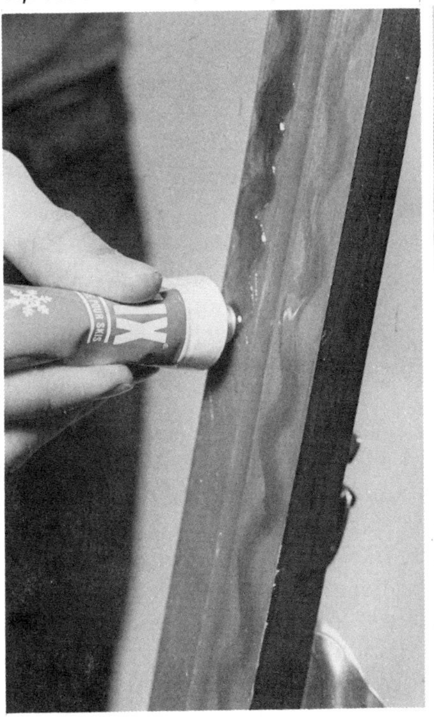

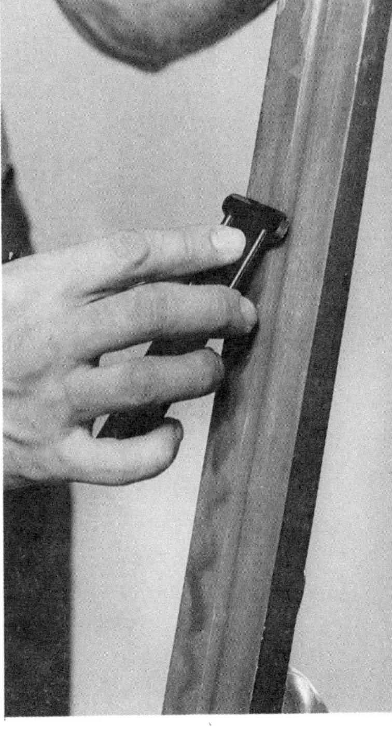

out with a spreader. If you wax outside, you need a torch for spreading. If it runs over the side of the ski, you've put too much on; mop up the excess with a rag.

Klister wax comes in a can like hard wax but behaves like klister. Daub it on in distinct intervals of a couple of inches and be prepared for the festoons of wax attaching cannister to ski bottoms even at arm's length — a bubble gum riot. Less is more here; as a matter of fact less may still be too much. Smooth it out with a torch and rag or a cork never more to be used.

Where to put it? The middle of the ski is your waxing target. Put hard wax on the center 2 to 4 feet of the ski. Klister, since it's stickier and slower, doesn't demand as long a strip, usually 1½ to 3 feet is plenty.

Two-wax systems: If you're just getting started in skiing or don't want to face the array of waxes and klisters (or are color blind), you can ski very nicely using the two-wax systems now on the market. They're so reliable I've used them on long multi-week ski expeditions. They're simple to use: one wax for dry and powdery snow below freezing and one wax for wet and packing snow above. In the Swix system, "gold wax is for cold, silver is for slop." The waxes are formulated to respond to a wide range of moisture and hardness in the snow: so even with only two waxes you get adequate performance. The secret is a subtle application of layers. Apply them thinly and cork them in well for cold dry snow. Be sparing in your first application, and if the skis are still slipping as the day warms, continue to add more wax. You get more grip not by switching to a different wax but by adding a thicker, rougher, longer coat. When the conditions get really slushy, you may have to apply up to a quarter to a half cannister of wet wax to get adequate grip.

A paper-thin layer of cold-snow wax, polished well with a waxing cork, works like hard green wax. A long, thick, unpolished layer of the same wax works like hard purple. A thin layer of wet-snow wax works like hard red, while a thick layer works about like red klister, but only on the flat. If you need real climbing grip in old slushy snow, you'd better use some regular red klister.

You can start each day of skiing by waxing with cold-snow wax at home; add warmer wax out on the trail, if

TWO WAX SYSTEM

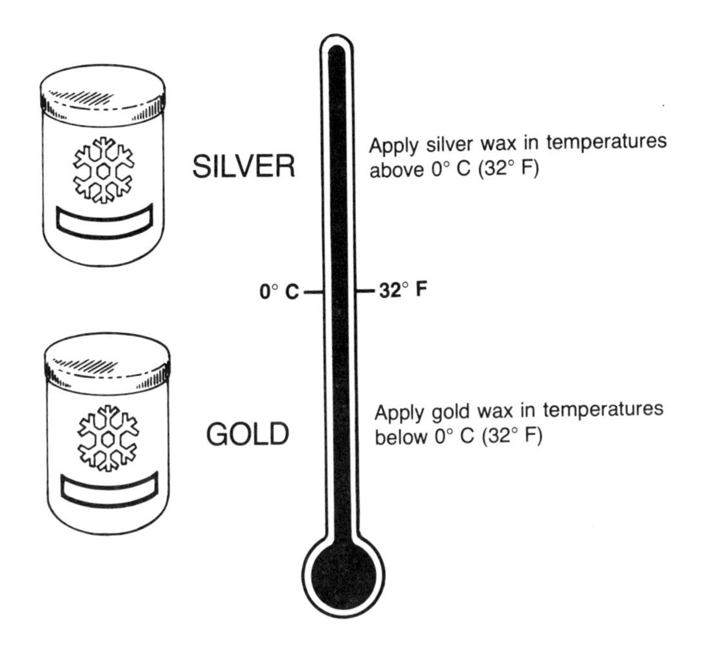

Information courtesy Swix Wax Company

necessary. For good kick, don't hesitate to wax the entire bottom of either wood or plastic skis with cold-snow wax. Wet wax is usually required only on the center 3 to 4 feet of the ski.

Because two-wax systems are very forgiving as snow hardness changes radically at the freezing point (the ultimately frustrating waxing temperature) and tend not to ice up as readily as regular wax, they work excellently in 32°F./0°C. snow and in snow lying on unfrozen ground, which is common in cities and southern areas. You can ski around Central Park in New York City, then head to Vermont or Colorado and use the same waxing system — it's adaptable. In difficult waxing conditions, even racers use it. After you become comfortable with the two-wax system you might want to try a little finer tuning by moving into the full waxing spectrum.

Wax removal and ski purification: Remove as much wax as possible with a scraper, working from tail to tip so that you roll up a ball of wax. If you're out on the trail, this is as much cleaning as you'll have to do. Otherwise, to prevent buildup of old waxes, scrape and then use a solvent or commercial wax remover with a rag. You can also use a torch to melt the wax and wipe it away, but be cautious and keep the torch moving so you don't melt the base of the ski.

Troubleshooting: If your skis are slippery and do not climb, your wax is too hard, you didn't put enough of it on, or what you did might have worn off. Before you make adjustments, make sure you've skied a couple of hundred yards so the wax gets cooled off and skied in. (Skis should be set outside after waxing and allowed to cool off.) Begin by adding a longer kicker of the same wax, especially in soft tracks filling in with snow or bushwhacking in deep snow. Then go to a light application of the next warmer wax.

If your skis do not glide, you may have put on too much wax or too soft a wax, sometimes creating an instant 6-inch platform of snow underfoot. Scrape and go to a colder wax.

When in doubt select a harder wax; you can put soft wax over hard for more grip, not vice versa. Do you ever put peanut butter over jelly on bread?

On a tour where you'll encounter variable snowônditons, wax for the coldest, dryest snow you'll ski through. Remember it's better to slip in the sunny meadow than stick in the shady forest.

To prevent wax from wearing off, there are a couple of solutions. The simplest is to heat the first layer into the ski base with a torch or iron, smoothing it out with a rag, to create a good bond. Set the skis outside to cool, then cork the next layer in.

If the snow is icy and abrasive, take the time to use klister wax's even stickier cousin, binder wax. Dab it on cautiously or freeze it outside and you'll be able to crayon it on. Smooth it out thinly with a warm iron or torch and cork; then apply a layer of hard wax, mixing it in while the binder is still a little warm. Set the skis outside and carefully cork in an additional layer or two of hard wax. It can't be denied that this is a tedious and difficult process; get some help the first time. But it's worth the trouble because

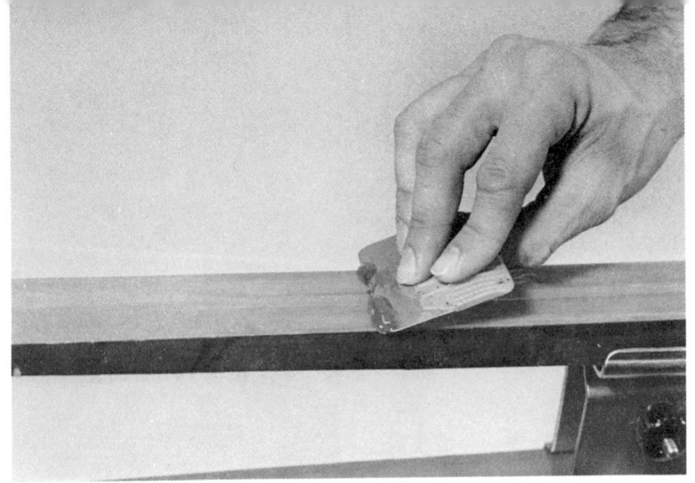

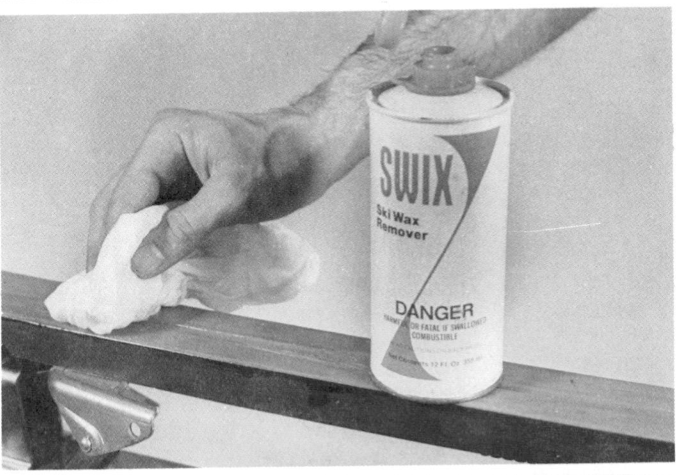

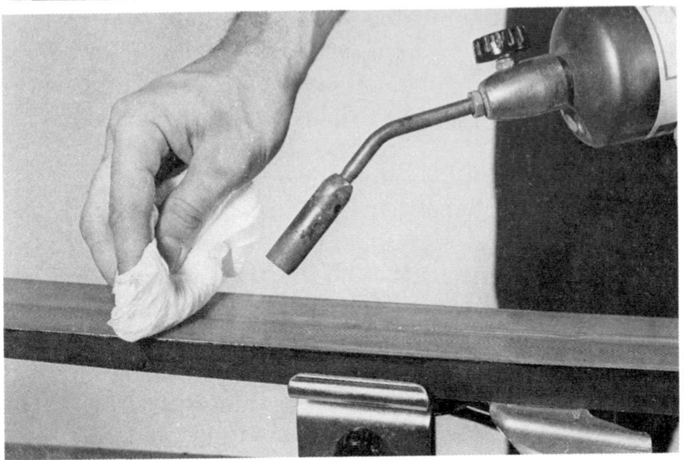

Scrape off old wax, then wipe clean with a rag and solvent or torch. (Peter Miller)

Here's a clever way to adjust your wax without taking your skis off. (Peter Miller)

you will get better climb uphill and not have to stop in mid-tour to rewax.

Purple and red hard waxes can get pretty gummy if crayoned on warm. Instead stroke them on gently in one direction when the wax is cold.

If you still have plenty of wax on at the end of the day's tour and snow conditions will be the same the next day, go with your old wax.

Beginners usually complain about slippery skis; for them a longer kicker of grip wax is a good idea. More expert skiers wail about slow skis; they'll want to experiment with the length, position, and thickness of the kicker and even get to know the different characteristics of the same color wax in different brands. Don't be reticent about asking questions — that's the best way to learn. The best way to experiment is to wax each ski differently; you can always adjust the less adequate ski out on the trail.

Wax in anticipation for the day's conditions — especially true for spring skiing. If it's 20 degrees early in the morning but will warm up to 50 at noon, calling for red klister, put the red on early instead of working up through blue and purple. Otherwise you're letting yourself in for a Hieronymous Bosch klister klassic.

A good wax job is worth the effort. Students who have switched skis with Trapp instructors are usually astonished at how smoothly they glide and how little effort is needed to ski on them.

Zero degree frustration: When snow falls at the freezing point, it occasions what is known as a "wax day." Which is not to say that you'll use wax, but that you may use fourteen or so in various combinations. Frustration is the order of the day and madness not far off. People are not amused by a Trapp instructor who throws up his hands and says, "I don't know," to a question about the wax most suitable for this sleazy, incorrigible, wayward, coy, devilish snow.

Why? As the temperature approaches 32°F./0°C. the snow decreases in hardness. Because there is less snow crystal penetration, you need a softer wax. At and around 32°F./0°C. the rate of change of snow crystal hardness is so accelerated that for every tenth of a degree of temperature change, the snow hardness changes manyfold. Since no wax composition can keep up with this rate of change of snow hardness, you need many different waxes for small changes in temperature (and a lot of patience).

Speed Waxes

You can ski quite well without paying attention to either the tips or tails of your skis, but even better if you take the time to pamper them with a little wax, thus adding performance and durability to the skis.

Plastic ski bases are either porous like polyethylene bases on higher-performance skis or nonporous like ABS bases on many recreational skis. Hard, nonporous materials will become faster with base waxing, but since the wax does not penetrate into the bottom, it wears off quickly and in my opinion is not worth your effort. Porous bases with brand names P-tex, Kofix, Fastex, etc., are prepared at the factories for maximum wax holding, resulting in a base with an appearance that is dry, rough, and hairy.

How to base prep: *Step 1:* For brand-new skis, use a metal scraper to eliminate excess hairs left from factory grinding. Be careful not to gouge the plastic.

Step 2: Hot waxing. Place the skis on a level bench with the bases up. Heat a waxing iron with a torch or, better, use an electric iron set at "wool." Choose a soft red or purple glider wax or equivalent Alpine wax for maximum saturation. Press the wax against the iron, dripping a line along each side of the groove, leaving the center 60-80 cm unwaxed to aid adhesion of the running grip wax which will be put there. Avoid heating the wax so much that it smokes.

Step 3: Smooth out the wax by running the iron back and forth over the base. Keep the iron moving or you'll melt the plastic or cause a delamination. Allow the wax to cool for about 15 minutes.

Step 4: Scrape excess wax off the base with a plastic scraper that will not damage the bottom. Don't forget to remove excess wax from the groove with a rounded plastic item like the head of a klister spreader and to clean up drippings on the sidewall. The final result should be a smooth base from which all paraffin seems to have been removed. Wax that has actually penetrated the plastic base is all that is left.

How often? As an ordinary tour skier, once or twice a year is adequate, unless you see the tips and tails begin to look white and dried out or you feel you are slower on downhills than your friends. Top international racers will base prep a new pair of skis several times before using them to ensure total saturation of the base for maximum speed.

How to speed wax: Just as you wax the middle of the ski according to the snow conditions for grip, so do you vary the speed wax on tips and tails for maximum glide. The process is similar to base prepping except now there are no excess hairs to be scraped. Racers and fast recreational skiers may change their speed wax daily; other skiers will not appreciate the performance difference enough to warrant the extra preparation time. There is no doubt that speed wax adds tremendously to your speed, especially in wet snow conditions. This is particularly true in stiff racing skis which ride only on the speed wax of tips and tails

Base prepping, steps 1-5 (left to right): Scraping base smooth. Melting wax. Smoothing. Scraping excess wax. Scraping the groove. (Peter Miller)

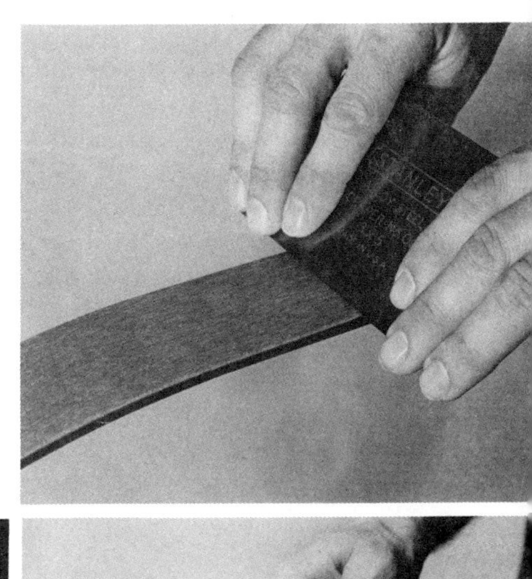

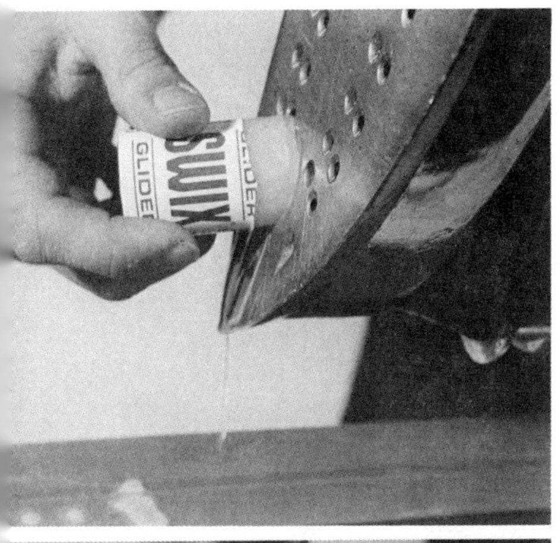

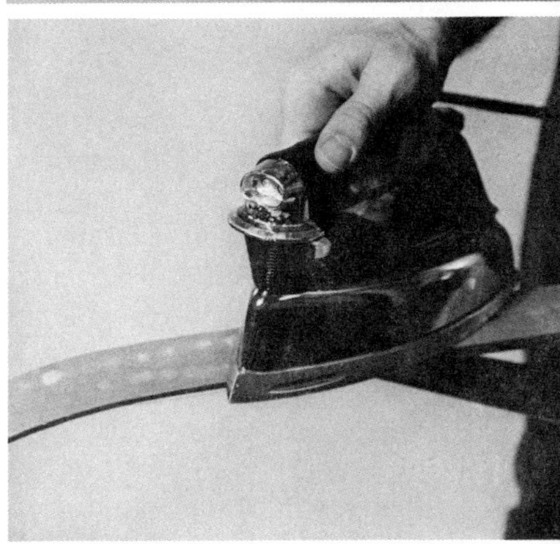

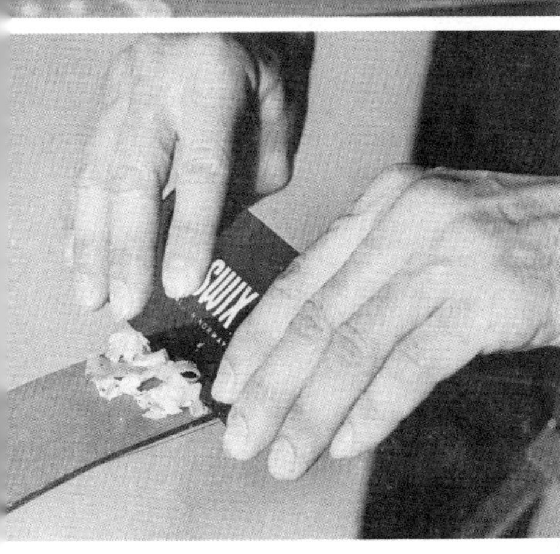

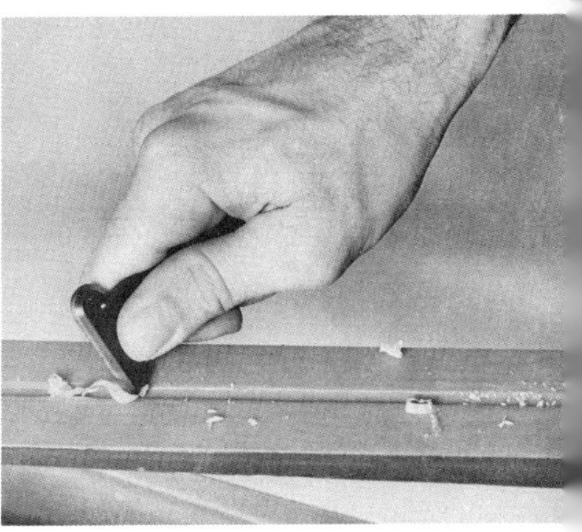

when going downhill. The special design of racing skis actually keeps the center gripping section up off the snow to reduce drag and increase speed.

Although you can use the same speed wax that Alpine skiers use, it can get pretty complicated. It's a lot easier to use the special X-C gliders color-coded to the gripping wax. Don't hesitate to mix them together. For instance, green glider seems to work well only on very cold snow. If you're using green wax for grip, you may want to mix blue and green gliders. The length of your glider is determined by the length of your kicking zone; hot wax only where you're not going to place your kicker wax.

If you're the kind of skier who likes to have a fast ski with plenty of glide, you may be interested in some waxing news from the 1979 Pre-Olympics at Lake Placid. Temperatures were extremely cold, on the order of minus 10°F., and made the snow feel like sandpaper under skis. Oddvar Braa, the dominant skier of the games, seemed to have the fastest skis of all. Apparently he mixed polar wax (for grip) and purple glider the length of the ski. "Polar and purple" not only slides off the tongue but slides down the hill pretty quickly as well and grips tremendously. The polar is an obvious choice, the purple improbable, as it was designed as a glider for much warmer snow. But as Harold Bjerke of Swix says, "Purple has turned out to be a glider with an incredibly wide range." So on extremely cold snow, try mixing glider in with your kicker wax to get a faster ski. Some wild experimentation may produce some pretty startling and satisfying results.

Ned Gillette. (Peter Miller)

THE LAST WORD

Skiing has been the cornerstone of my life, not by design but through a natural evolution that began when my father held my three-year-old person between his legs and cruised downhill. For a long time I figured skiing should stay just that — playful cruising. I tried the strict business world, but skis seemed to appear under the desk. When cross-country skiing really began to take off in the United States, I found myself in a position to grow with it, combining athletics, creativity, business, adventure, contact with wonderful people, and a substantial amount of time spent outdoors. Serious enjoyment seems to slide along with my skis, and I hope it will with yours too.

So if this book has started you off on the right foot or enhances your acquaintance with skiing as an old friend, made you laugh a bit at other beginners' trials and tribulations, allowed you to experience the joys and sorrows of expeditions, and broadened your perspective on the endless opportunities that skiing can bring to you as families, tourers, racers or adventurers, then the writing has been worthwhile.

On the other hand, perhaps you need one last bit of encouragement . . .

...TANDEM SKIING!

Want to revitalize your skiing, gain new appreciation for the kick turn, and put new demands on your coordination? Get an old pair of long skis and mount two sets of bindings. Skiing on the flat is giddy enough, but downhilling is positively thrilling — a twin telemark feels like driving an 18-wheeler down a 10 percent grade. If you're having trouble picking up the rhythm or dropping into a telemark, try a pair of tandems — you'll have no choice but to get the technique right — as rather graphically demonstrated on the following pages.

(Peter Miller)

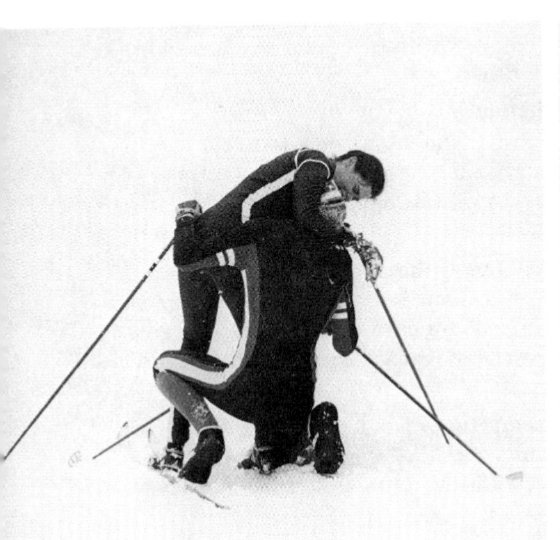

Books from The Mountaineers include:

Cross-Country Ski Gear

Complete technical information on the design, construction, care and use of all types of cross-country ski equipment, including skis, poles, bindings and accessories. By Michael Brady, ski industry consultant and internationally published author on cross-country skiing.

Medicine for Mountaineering

A handbook for treating accidents and illnesses in remote areas, where a physician may be several days away. Includes treatment of traumatic and environmental injuries and diseases, with particular emphasis on illnesses of high altitude or a hostile environment.

Rock Climbing

A how-to-book by Peter Livesey, one of the world's best-known rock climbers, written for the general reader. Step by step through all the latest techniques and state-of-the-art equipment. Outstanding instructional photos.

Snowshoeing

Complete information on techniques for safe, enjoyable travel in any terrain or weather; how to select, care for and use snowshoe equipment. By Gene Prater.

The ABC of Avalanche Safety

How to spot potential avalanche areas, how to avoid one in mountain travel, how to survive if caught, how to rescue others — a handy pocket guide by Edward LaChapelle.

Mountaineering First Aid

Compact handbook for dealing with remote-area accidents and helping to prevent them. Excellent text for outdoor safety or first-aid classes. Covers immediate care for common emergencies, plus preparation for rescue or evacuation. By Dick Mitchell.

Mountains of the World

All the major mountains and hundreds of out-of-the-way peaks and ranges, from the Alps to Antarctica, from Everest to Ecuador, from the Cascades to the Caucasus. Route descriptions, history, local color by William Bueler.

The Mountains of Canada

Over 100 magnificent color photos by some of the most talented photographers in North America. Author Randy Morse, himself a climber, sees mountains in terms of their relationship to modern man. He includes, to counterpoint the photos, fascinating stories of climbers as they faced the challenge of these peaks.

K2 — The Savage Mountain

The second highest mountain in the world long withheld its summit from American climbers. Probably the best remembered expedition to K2 was in 1953, led by Charles Houston and Robert Bates. They told the engrossing story in this classic of mountaineering literature. This reprint also includes retrospective essays by expedition members.

Gervasutti's Climbs

The autobiography of one of the leading Italian mountaineers of the 1930s, who made many first ascents in the Western Alps. Gervasutti writes with a depth of detail, yet with a degree of introspection that will interest mountaineers of all generations.

The Last Blue Mountain

The mountain was Haramosh, a lesser known but thoroughly challenging peak in the Himalaya. The expedition was an adventurous reconnaissance until, suddenly, a fall through a cornice led to a series of incredible disasters. This book leads to a nerve-wrenching conclusion you'll never forget. By Ralph Barker.

Tales of A Western Mountaineer

Complete reprint of a rare (1924) account by C.E. Rusk, who made a number of first-ascents on Northwest mountains and named major glaciers on Mt. Adams and Glacier Peak.

The Unknown Mountain

A mountain literature classic, long out of print: Don Munday's story of the discovery and exploration of ice-tipped Mt. Waddington and other peaks of the B.C. Coast Range. These trips were made in the 1920s and 1930s, through rugged unmapped terrain, without benefit of today's lightweight gear.

100 Hikes in the Alps

A well-illustrated guide to the best hikes in a number of Alpine valleys, in Yugoslavia, Austria, Italy, France, Switzerland and Germany, plus selected areas of the Pyrenees. Maps, photos.

. . .plus regional hiking and climbing guides on Washington, British Columbia and Alaska

For a complete list of books, write The Mountaineers, 719 Pike Street, Seattle, Washington 98101.